A WILTSHIRE MOONRAKER

A WILTSHIRE MOONRAKER

Margaret Wood

ISIS
LARGE PRINT
Oxford

First published in Great Britain 2007
by ISIS Publishing Ltd.

Published in Large Print 2007 by ISIS Publishing Ltd.,
7 Centremead, Osney Mead, Oxford OX2 0ES
by arrangement with
the Author

British Library Cataloguing in Publication Data
Wood, Margaret
    A Wiltshire moonraker. – Large print ed.
    (Isis reminiscence series)
    1. Wood, Margaret – Childhood and youth
    2. Large type books
    3. Swindon (England) – Biography
    I. Title
    942.3'13'092

ISBN 978–0–7531–9448–5 (hb)
ISBN 978–0–7531–9449–2 (pb)

20179852 Printed and bound in Great Britain by
T.J. International Ltd., Padstow, Cornwall

DEDICATION

To the memory of my father and my mother.

CONTENTS

FOREWORD

Swindon, in the 1930s, was a typical small industrial town which relied on the Great Western Railway Company to provide the majority of employment for its inhabitants and for its economic existence and eventual growth.

Isambard Kingdom Brunel put Swindon on the map by choosing this midway point of his rail connection between London and Bristol as a watering hole for his thirsty steam-horses, not to mention their passengers. This autobiography, of a member of one of Swindon's families, gives a vivid and accurate insight into working class life during the first half of the 20th century and the changes which have taken place in Swindon, and in society in general, since then.

ACKNOWLEDGEMENTS

I would like to thank my daughter, Deirdre, for her help and encouragement and for undertaking the tedious task of proof-reading.

I wish to thank my sister, Win, for her help in "jogging my memory" regarding some of the events of our childhood.

PART ONE

THE FIRST DECADE

CHAPTER ONE

The Early Years

"Come and see what your Mummy has got for you."

These were the words with which a good neighbour, Mrs Webber, woke my sisters to announce my arrival. It was the morning of the 8th July 1930 and I had been born during the night, to my dear parents Geoffrey and Teresa Wood. As was common in those days, particularly among working class families of which we were one, it had been a home birth with neighbours and a midwife in attendance. My sisters, Kathleen aged nine and a half and Winifred aged seven, had slept peacefully through the commotion. What is even more surprising is that neither had any idea that Mum was pregnant. So much for sex education in the 1930s — it was nonexistent!

"Well, what do you think?" asked Mum.

"She's beautiful. What's her name?" my sisters replied.

"Well, we thought we'd call her Margaret but you can choose her second name."

There was some deliberation but eventually total agreement between the two older girls:

"Lilian," they announced.

How many times have I regretted their choice. I hate the name. Funnily enough both Kath and Win later admitted that they didn't know why they chose it because neither of them liked it much either.

I should not have complained. My next older sister had been named after her paternal grandmother (as was the custom) and had to endure Winifred or rather Winnie for short. She would so much have preferred to be called Josephine, her second name. Despite Mum's insistence that we all three had good solid names and that they were not to be shortened, as we grew up Kathleen became Kath and Winnie became Win. Funnily enough I have always remained Margaret to my family and friends.

So it was that I made my arrival into this working class family and, despite my father's disappointment at yet another daughter when he had always wanted a son, my parents were overjoyed at the birth of their third daughter and the completion of their family.

Times were hard in the 1930s, not least because of the aftermath of the 1920 General Strike and the First World War but also because of the Great Depression of 1930. Luckily my father, a skilled worker, was fortunate to remain in employment (although often on short time) during these depressing times.

My mother, of course, never worked. Like many husbands my father felt that "a woman's place was in the home." My mother seemed happy to fulfil this role and was always there when we girls (or my father) needed her.

I guess my next recollection must be of life around the age of three years. We lived in a three-bedroom terrace house which had been newly built when my parents moved into it in 1925. My father was a trainee draughtsman with the Midland and South Western Railway Company in Cirencester before I was born. He had served his apprenticeship as a fitter and turner but been given the opportunity to train for a "white collar" job in this relatively small railway company.

In 1925 the firm was bought up by the Great Western Railway Company and my father had to move to Swindon where the main railway works were situated. Having a wife and young family to support he opted for the better paid manual work and reverted to being a fitter, turner and erector for GWR (lovingly referred to as "God's Wonderful Railway" by the loyal workers). He bought his first house, 9 Bruce Street, where I was born, for £375 — a staggering amount in those days and one which was made possible only through a company mortgage scheme.

Being only 10 minutes walk away from the factory gates, many of our neighbours worked "inside" as it was called when one was employed by the major employer in the town — the GWR. There were considerable benefits for working for such a new and large organisation, not least the family membership of the GWR Medical Fund, the forerunner of the National Health Service. Mum must have been eternally grateful for this fringe benefit as she nursed all three children through the usual childhood illnesses, scarlet fever, whooping cough, measles, mumps. Immunisation was in its infancy at that time.

One particular day, I recall, I was playing on the floor of the living room whilst Mum stood ironing and chatting with our next-door neighbour, Mrs. Stafford. Adult chat can be so boring for a child, especially one as hungry as me. Eventually, Mrs. Stafford announced she had better "go and get Bill's tea" — her husband, also a railway worker, would soon be home from work. My joy at her departure and the prospect of Mum preparing our tea could not be contained.

"Good," I said.

Mum gave me a look which said "Just you wait, my girl" but ignored the remark, hoping that Mrs. Stafford had not heard. As she left the house I followed her and slammed the door behind her.

"That will teach her to outstay her welcome," I thought.

Mum was furious.

"Don't you ever do that again, my girl, or you will feel the back of my hand. How could you be so rude to a good neighbour. Now you will wait for your tea."

At the time I couldn't see what all the fuss was about but I guess this was my first lesson in being polite — even to someone who I considered to be a bit of a nuisance.

My pre-school years passed in a haze of outings to town, or to the fields in autumn to pick blackberries with Mum and at least one of the neighbours. But I also remember vividly the boring days in bed when I was ill, usually with a sore throat. Many children were quite sickly in their early years and I was no exception. Mum gave me as much of her time as she could whilst I was in bed sick, but a home to run with no "mod-cons" left precious little spare time. Maybe that was why, when I spent a boring hour peeling wallpaper from the bedroom wall, my parents were not really angry. Dad just got on with the redecorating as usual.

Most of all I remember evenings and weekends when the family was together. Of course there was no television but we had a wireless which Mum and Dad listened to avidly. At five o'clock each weekday there was "Children's Hour" with presenter Uncle Mac. I listened to this every day. My favourite programme was "Toy Town" but I also listened weekly to the Ovaltinies and I became a Gold Badge member of their club (probably because Mum saved the coupons from the Ovaltine tin and sent away for the badges). After tea, Mum would sit knitting and allow me to unpin her long hair and play at hairdressers. I can see her face now as she winced with an "Ouch" when I pulled too much. But she continued to allow me to plait and curl her hair, using rags as curlers.

In no time at all it seemed, I was approaching five years of age and it was time to start school. I must have started at the local school, Even Swindon Infants, after Easter in 1935, just before I was five years old. Mum was having no nonsense about whether I wanted to go to school. I was sent off on the first day with a neighbour's daughter who, being about twelve years old, was "in the big school."

My recollections of my first class are of a short, fat teacher called Miss Ellis. She was kind and jovial but quite strict. She seemed to waddle around and didn't seem to do much exercise during PE lessons. The head teacher was Miss Ninnis — tall and thin with her hair in a bun, like my Mum. These two reminded me of my Aunts Poppie and Freda. Poppie was tall and thin, Freda short and fat.

Lunchtime was from 12 noon to 2 o'clock so naturally I went home for lunch. After lunch we returned for "rest period". Children who had started school earlier, at four years, were settled on rush mats on the floor of the classroom or in the hall, for an hour's sleep. We older children — those nearly five years old and "ready for school" — were merely expected to sit with our head on our arms on the desk for a short period. It seemed like an eternity to me but I was so grateful that I was grown up enough not to be forced to lie on a mat and go to sleep when it wasn't bedtime!

My other vivid memory is of milk time, which was mid-morning, before we went out to play in the playground for some fifteen minutes break.

"Now who is going to be milk monitor this week?" Miss Ellis would enquire on a Monday morning. Hands would shoot up. Not mine. I was much too shy, yet I would have loved the privilege and responsibility.

"Let's see, Margaret, I don't think you have done it yet," said Miss Ellis, "That's it then, it's Margaret's turn this week."

I was overjoyed at the prospect. My duty was to make sure that the crate of milk was delivered to the classroom by the caretaker well before the end of the lesson. Then I had to supervise the pupils leaving their desks, one row at a time, collecting their one-third of a pint bottle of milk and a straw and returning to their desk to drink it.

"No drinking on the way back to your place," I was able to remonstrate with offenders. Afterwards empty bottles had to be returned to the crate and the cardboard top of the bottle and the used straw put in the wastepaper basket. No-one could leave the classroom for the playground until all was neat and tidy.

The responsibility was awesome!

On cold, winter days, the milk monitor was allowed to put the milk on top of the radiators as soon as it arrived so that by the time playtime arrived, the milk was warm. I hated warm milk and often bribed the milk monitor to forget one bottle and leave it in the crate for me. If the milk was late arriving there was not time to put it on the radiators and we often had to drink iced milk. I much preferred that.

Even Swindon School was typical of the local school at which all children of the neighbourhood would attend. Free education was available for all children between the ages of 5 and 14 years and schools which catered for all ages ("all through schools") were situated relevant to areas of population. The school buildings were often relics of the Victorian era and sometimes in need of repair. Classes were large — 40 or even 50 pupils were not uncommon. Sometimes two classes shared one classroom. There were only outside toilets and little in the way of equipment, gymnasiums or playing fields.

Children started school at five years of age, occasionally a little younger if the school was not oversubscribed. At the age of seven years they transferred from the Infants department to the Juniors where they remained until the dreaded scholarship (a grammar school entrance test), the outcome of which decided their fate for the completion of their school years. Pass it and you got to grammar school; fail and you remained at the same school but transferred to the senior section — standards 6 and 7.

Children who, by their success at this grammar school test, were deemed to be intelligent transferred to grammar schools where the curriculum extended to include mathematics, English language and literature, history, geography, sciences (biology, chemistry and physics), and languages both classical and modern. Physical Education was taught in well-equipped gymnasiums and each school had a playing field where team games such as hockey, tennis, netball, football and cricket were taught.

For those who failed the grammar school test and remained at the Elementary School, the curriculum was very narrow, consisting mainly of the 3Rs (arithmetic being the only aspect of mathematics which was taught). Some geography and history was studied but no sciences. Arts and crafts lessons consisted mainly of drawing or painting. Once a week girls spent a day doing cookery, housewifery and needlework, whilst the boys did woodwork. Physical education was dependent upon the facilities available. Although most schools could teach netball to the girls by using the school playground, the rest of the physical education lessons were mainly forms of drill.

One of my earliest recollections of Infant School was knitting lessons. I suspect I was in the second year of school — about six years old. One afternoon the teacher announced, "We're all going to learn to knit."

The girls whooped with joy; the boys groaned.

"Why can't we do woodwork?" they chorused.

No reason was forthcoming, but the boys soon accepted their fate. Anything was better than sums or spelling! Each child was given two short wooden needles on to which a few stitches had been placed and the first row of knitting completed. With instructions on how to hold the needles the teacher demonstrated, "In, round, through and off; in, round, through and off."

Success was spasmodic. A few of the girls got the idea but pulled the wool so tightly that the next row was impossible. Others had such loose stitches that they kept falling off the needles. Most of the boys were unsuccessful, due mainly to a total lack of enthusiasm, although the sight of a few with tongues lolling out of the sides of their mouths suggested a modicum of concentration. As for me — I was totally bored. You see, my mother had taught me to knit when I was about three years old. I was already knitting my own dolls' clothes and was currently engaged on a simple jacket for a neighbour's forthcoming baby.

"Please, Miss, I can already knit," I tried to explain.

"Good," replied the flustered teacher, whose rapid progress round the class to retrieve dropped stitches, correct hand movements and so forth made teaching knitting to a class of 40 plus six year olds a daunting task. "You just keep knitting — just plain garter stitch mind, and I'll come and show you how to cast off as soon as I'm free."

The lesson progressed. For me it was line after boring line of garter stitch. At last I plucked up the courage to explain, "Please, Miss, I can cast off on my own."

"All right, go ahead." I don't think the teacher really believed me.

For the second lesson I was put in charge of giving out the previous week's attempts, to which each child had attached a name tag. I was proud to be knitting monitor — I wasn't "pushy" enough to become monitor of anything else on a regular basis. The teacher was impressed by the work I had done the previous lesson and now asked me if I would go around the class with her and help those who had not quite grasped the art. This was certainly an improvement on my first week's lesson but being the teacher's helper does not endear one to one's peers, so I asked the teacher if I might bring in my own knitting for next lesson instead of doing what the others did.

"All right, just this once, but next week I'll be teaching the class how to cast on so I expect you will want to join in."

"I can already cast on."

I was beginning to sound precocious but I was not prepared for another boring lesson, nor was I prepared to suffer the taunts of "teacher's pet" after the lesson. The next lesson arrived and I quietly got on with my own knitting — the simple baby's jacket. After a while the teacher had time to inspect my work. I was knitting in a very simple pattern which involved a row of holes about every sixth line. The teacher seemed amazed.

"How did you get those holes?" she enquired. I looked at her in disbelief. She surely didn't mean than she didn't know how to do a row of holes. I had had to learn that very early on in my training when I had to make a row through which to thread the ribbon of a pair of baby's mittens.

"You just knit one, make one, and knit two together," I explained.

"Show me," she demanded. I really don't think she believed I was capable. The next time I came to a "pattern" row, I called her over and demonstrated.

"Go and fetch Miss Innes," she instructed.

Miss Innes was the head teacher. She was a strict but kindly lady. Oh dear, I thought, I'm for it now. What have I done? I don't understand. My Mum said my knitting was good. Miss Innes arrived. As was the custom, every child stood up as she entered the classroom. The repercussions on their knitting were disastrous. The next half hour was spent retrieving dropped stitches.

"Sit down, everyone. How nice to see such a busy class," Miss Innes commented.

My teacher then said, "I've brought you here to see Margaret's knitting."

Miss Innes duly inspected the work whilst my teacher explained my already acquired ability and the help I had been with the beginners in the class. Miss Innis complimented me and quizzed me, asking, "When did you learn to knit? Who taught you? What are you making? What else have you made?" The questions seemed endless.

I should have been proud to be singled out in such a way but all I could think was "Why all the fuss?" The whole episode was dismissed when I merely reported to my Mum, "Guess what, Mum, none of the children in my class can cast on and off. In fact most couldn't even knit until Miss showed them how."

Even Swindon school acted very much as a community school since virtually all children spent their entire school life within its walls. It did its best to provide extra-curricular activities and often produced plays or musicals with as many of the pupils as possible being included in the cast. Many photographs of my sisters' involvement in such productions indicate the enthusiasm with which the pupils participated. I suspect many of the costumes were made by the mothers of the pupils. I know that my mother was extremely handy with a needle and thread! The apparent lavishness of these productions belies the real poverty which was evident in many households.

My own encounter with dramatic productions at school came quite early in my education. I must have been about seven years old when the teacher announced, "We have decided to put on a play."

I can't remember the exact title but it must have been along the lines of Alice in Wonderland. There was a Queen of Hearts and a Knave of Hearts to be cast and I had my eye on the Queen's part.

"Tomorrow we shall have a practice run and several of you will get the chance to read the parts of the main characters," announced the teacher.

I could hardly sleep that night. Tomorrow was to be my "big day". I knew that I was capable of playing the Queen. I appreciated some of my friends were also quite competent performers but I was good at reading, so would not stumble over my words. The day of the "auditions" arrived.

"Now, who wants to read for the part of the Queen?" asked the teacher.

Mine was one of several hands to shoot up. We all had an equal chance. So sure was I that I had landed the part that I did not bother to offer to read for other parts. We were told that decisions would be made in the light of the auditions and that we would know the full cast the next day.

I sat quite complacently the next day whilst the teacher began the long list of parts which had been cast.

"The Queen of Hearts — Joan James," she announced.

I couldn't believe my ears. In my opinion Joan hadn't read the part very well and certainly she wasn't as pretty as me. How could they? Had they forgotten I

15

read the part? The rest of the cast followed in a blur. To say I was disappointed was putting it mildly. I was relegated to a member of the chorus — a singing part at that. Didn't they know I was almost tone-deaf. I didn't like singing. I wanted to be a famous actress.

That first encounter with dramatic art and particularly with auditions was to stand me in good stead for the future. It taught me not to take things for granted; it made me realise other people were talented; it taught me the danger of being over-presumptuous; in a small way it taught me humility.

CHAPTER
TWO

The Grandmothers —
Chalk and Cheese

My paternal grandmother was a severe woman. One might describe her as "Victorian". Everything had to be correct. Children were certainly expected to be "seen and not heard". Visits to Granny Wood were a sort of penance for me. Fortunately I was taken there only on day outings. I never remember having to stay overnight. Granny Wood was a widow. Her husband Anthony had died before I was born and Granny had moved into an almshouse. In her later years (she lived well into her eighties) she suffered from dementia and visits became quite a nightmare, although eventually Poppie and Freda, her daughters, returned from "service" to care for their mother.

Granny Wood insisted that "the devil found work for idle hands". If I began to fidget, I was shown how to link the fingers of my two hands together and rotate the thumbs. I still do it to this day if I'm bored. How pathetic! It hasn't stopped the devil finding work for me!

"I'm bored. What can I do?" I complained to my mother on one such visit.

"Ssh!" was the muted reply. But dear old Granny had heard, despite her protestations of being deaf — when she didn't want to hear, I might add.

"Take off your stocking and play with your shoe" was Granny's advice.

I looked at her with incredulity. I wore socks, not stockings. I had also received a clip round the ear in church one Sunday when, during a rather boring sermon, I had taken off my shoe.

"I don't understand," I complained. Granny's knowing smile was supposed to enlighten me to the joke but on a five-year old the humour was lost.

Eventually I was given a ball and told to go outside to play. Can you imagine the mayhem one small child can create in the communal gardens of a row of almshouses? A ball needing to be retrieved from a neighbour's garden was greeted with frantic taps on the window and gestures to "get off." Throwing the ball against the wall got the neighbours out of their doors with complaints about the "thud, thud" of the ball.

"What do these old people do all day?" I contemplated, "Sit at their windows waiting for me to arrive and come out to play?"

My sisters being older and, by nature or education, better behaved than I was, were expected to sit indoors listening in silence to the grown-up chit chat. The one redeeming factor of such visits was a little game called "The Road to Berlin" which Grannie allowed us to play with. It was one of those games of skill of hand

18

movement and control where one was expected to move a little metal ball over a glass-covered wooden map which was scattered with holes. The object was to negotiate the ball from the bottom to the top (Leipzig to Berlin) without losing it down a hole. I'm sure that was one of the ways in which my sisters learned patience and self-discipline. When I was eventually allowed to play with it, I found it was all I could do to refrain from unladylike expletives within five minutes of handling the precious map. That game is still in one piece today, some century after it was bought, but no thanks to me.

Afternoon tea with Granny Wood was a nightmare.

"Sit still." "Tuck your elbows in." "Don't 'choke' your knife." "Use your serviette." The remonstrations were endless. Tea was served in the best china cups which began their journey next to the teapot on a lace-covered tea tray. How I managed to complete meals without spilling tea or dropping crumbs I do not know — probably because we were not encouraged to eat too much on such occasions.

As Granny's dementia increased she became, to me, quite amusing. One afternoon she looked lovingly at a vase of cut flowers on the table and remarked, "Oh, Geoffrey, you do look pretty in your new frock."

My maternal grandmother, Granny Stratford, was quite different. I barely remember her but my sisters describe her vividly.

My mother was one of ten children, five boys and five girls. Her father, a lamplighter by trade, died when Mum was very young so Granny Stratford had a very

19

hard life, bringing up nine surviving children on her own. They lived in a two-up, two-down cottage. Granny went out cleaning and took in washing to earn a few shillings but the family lived mostly "off the parish" — the charity of the local church. There was no social service at the turn of the 19th/20th centuries. Mum explained the help the parish gave by the example of ten loaves of bread being delivered each Monday. These were expected to feed the family for the whole week. By Sunday the bread was very stale but still eagerly eaten by children with little else to fill their stomachs. According to Mum, the family's diet was plain and boring but they were never hungry. A large pot of stew consisting of bones and vegetables was always simmering on the open fire. Granny Stratford was a genius at making a halfpenny worth of bacon scraps into a meal.

The children learned how to earn the odd copper or two of pocket money. They would run errands for neighbours, take back empty beer bottles and collect the halfpenny deposit from them. One of Mum's brothers used to take a neighbour's dog for walks to earn his pocket money. This was how Mum's sister got her name. She had been christened Philomena Annie Mary but her brothers called her "Dink" after the dog which they used to walk. That name stayed with her until her death. I only knew her as Auntie Dink. Indeed it was not until I saw her tombstone that I knew her full name.

Because of her hard life, and the fact that she was always surrounded by children, Granny Stratford had cultivated a sense of calm in the face of adversity. Everyone was welcome in her house, not least the grandchildren. I remember being given huge chunks of bread and dripping which I was allowed to eat whilst playing out in the street. Granny Stratford loved children and would often emerge from the house with a piece of old clothes line and insist on joining us in a game of skipping. She was a very rotund old lady and the sight of her skipping was something almost beyond imagination.

Mum told me many stories of her childhood. Her five brothers all slept in the attic. One can only imagine the mayhem they caused when confined to such a small area; but the girls were no angels. One Sunday afternoon, Granny had got the older girls ready for Sunday School and had allowed them outside to play whilst she concentrated on the younger ones. My mother and her sister Dink decided to remove their "tams" (large woolly hats) and fill them with grass, newly mown in the neighbouring field. The idea was to turn them into cushions so that they could sit more comfortably on the wire fence and enjoy a swing.

Plunging her hand into the mown grass, Dink managed to locate a broken bottle and the result was a severely cut arm.

"Oh, God, Mum will kill us!" she cried as the blood spilled over the clean white pinafore.

"Wait a minute," Mum replied. Taking off her own white apron, she wrapped it tightly around the wound and marched Dink home.

Apparently Granny Stratford was not amused, but treated the accident with her usual calm. A neighbour was called who, having a meagre knowledge of first aid, cleaned the wound and bound it up before Granny walked Dink, plus the other smaller offspring, all the way to the local cottage hospital where stitches were inserted. Sunday School was forgotten for that week but the cost of the required treatment ensured the incident remained in everyone's mind for a long time.

When I recall my two grandmothers, I realise the contrasts. Granny Wood, a petite, straight-backed lady was solemn and precise; Granny Stratford, short and fat with a jolly face, was always happy and welcoming. Granny Wood expected children to know their place; Granny Stratford loved children and made them the centre of any gathering, inventing games for them to play and joining in. At Granny Wood's, one was lucky to get half an apple or one biscuit; at Granny Stratford's one was welcome to share anything and everything she possessed. There was never much food, but there was lots of love and lots of fun.

CHAPTER
THREE

The Aunts

My father had two sisters, Poppie and Freda, both of whom remained spinsters all their life. I am not sure how Poppie got her name for she was christened Edith Maud but I only knew her as Auntie Poppie.

Both girls were older than my father and I learned later in my life that Freda was not his real sister. She had been one of illegitimate twins born to a close relative. Such was the stigma attached to illegitimacy in those days that the whole affair was hushed up by other members of the family adopting the twins and bringing them up as their own. It is sad to think that Freda, to my knowledge, never met her twin sister yet the latter was adopted by a family who lived only some twenty miles away.

As was the custom in working-class families, the girls were sent "into service" as soon as they left school. Freda eventually became a Cook and Poppie a Lady's Maid. I could listen for hours to their adventures whilst in service. Freda recalled how one evening the son of the master of the house, an arrogant young man, returned home in the late evening.

"Where's my dinner?" he enquired of his mother.

"We've already eaten," was the reply. "We thought you would not be returning this evening."

"Fetch Freda. I need my dinner," he demanded.

"But the servants will have eaten themselves and be preparing to retire by now."

"They are paid to serve, so tell them to fetch my dinner."

Freda was sent for and presented with the request, which obviously caused a dilemma. On returning to the kitchen she hit upon the solution. She went through the bin of "leftovers" which were destined for the pig's swill and retrieved sufficient to present, after suitable "washing down", as a full course dinner.

After satisfying his hunger the son became more tolerant and called for Freda.

"Well done! That was delicious," he commented.

Freda had a job to keep a straight face and by the time she had returned to the kitchen was in fits of laughter.

Both Poppie and Freda began their lives in service in lowly positions. From scullery maids they progressed to parlour maids, then to seamstresses. Freda was particularly good with her needle. She had excelled at needlework at school and the skills continued throughout her life. She made the night and day gowns for my first child when she was well past retirement age and embroidered them with delicate feather stitches. She was also an expert at crochet and made a variety of items, from milk bottle tops to blouses and even bedspreads.

Poppie was not as talented with needle and thread so eventually became a lady's maid. She was interested in nursing and, even without formal training, was ready and willing to administer to her ailing "ladies". She told tales of using leeches on the old people to reduce blood pressure.

Poppie changed her positions a number of times throughout her life in service. Being a lady's maid, her employers were usually elderly and often in poor health. As one died, so Poppie had to seek another position! Many of her "ladies" were extremely rich and she spent lots of time travelling the world. She often brought back mementos from those travels and I still cherish some of the African bead bracelets and dolls she brought me.

One lady she worked for had grandchildren about the same age as me. Occasionally Poppie would be given clothing which the granddaughter had outgrown. I was always delighted to receive these garments. They were so different from my usual clothes which were often handmade by my mother. I remember one beautiful white sweater which still had the nametag of the last owner, "Ann Coles", in it. I was so proud to have a name in my sweater, even though it wasn't mine, that I refused to let my mother take it out.

When Granny Wood became too old to look after herself, Freda and Poppie gave up their residential jobs to live at home and we visited them frequently. As a young girl I never tired of hearing of their exploits in service and particularly of Poppie's travels around the world. My greatest joy was to be allowed to rummage through her box of jewellery and small items she had brought back from her travels. Later my own daughter enjoyed the same treats on her rare visits to her Great Aunt Poppie.

Despite the poverty in which the family was brought up, Granny Stratford ensured all the boys were given a trade. She somehow got together the money to pay for apprenticeships so that each was quite capable of earning a living and bringing up their own families in relative luxury.

Although working class girls were normally destined for "service", Granny Stratford was reluctant to send her girls away. They all went (apart from Marty, the youngest) but few stayed any length of time. Mum spent only a month in service. Apparently she was so unhappy that Granny fetched her back home. Eventually three of them, Win, Marty and Mum, found work in a local draper's shop and lived at home.

Having four sisters and five brothers, my mother found it difficult to keep in touch with them all but the closest were Aunties Win, Dink, and Marty. Auntie Dink loved children, just like Granny Stratford. Sadly she had none of her own but managed to adopt a baby boy called Dick. She often spent a week or so with us during the summer and I remember her playing endlessly with Dick.

Apparently Win and Dink had never really got on. I don't know what the feud was about but I remember that if either visited us, the other kept well away. Auntie Dink was the second oldest of the girls and very independent. She eventually married a man from the north and they settled in Yorkshire. She soon became the typical outspoken "Yorkshire Lass". Nobody took advantage of her. Auntie Win was younger and, apparently, as a young girl had been rather a "whinger". The slightest ache or pain was a signal for her to be off work sick whilst her sisters were expected to "soldier on" to supplement the family purse. Being small in stature made Auntie Win quite bossy and probably the two girls were so alike in temperament that they were destined never to get on with each other.

Auntie Win was very tiny — about 4 ft 10 ins tall and rather plump. I remember her as "Little Auntie Win" who was married to Uncle Laurie, a jovial Welshman. Auntie Win and Uncle Laurie had three sons, just about the same ages as myself and my two sisters, so we grew up almost like brothers and sisters despite the fact that Auntie Win and Uncle Laurie lived most of their married life in London. As both my father and Uncle Laurie worked for the GWR, they had the privilege of cheap rail travel so we were able to visit each other quite frequently, and Auntie Win's three boys, George, Jim and Peter, spent many summer holidays with us in Swindon.

I loved my trips to London. It was such an exciting city despite Auntie Win's protestations of the wickedness it contained. I remember once being told not to loiter when walking in London.

"Never stand still," Auntie Win had instructed. "If I was to stand in the street, I can assure you some bad man would come up to me and try to take me off."

27

I might have only been nine years old at the time but I could not envisage any man wanting to "take off" this short, fat, bossy woman. Indeed had he tried so to do, Auntie would probably have jumped up and clipped him round the ears with her handbag.

Because Auntie Marty's husband left her when her only daughter, Monica, was just a baby, Mum and Dad took them under their wing and every Christmas the two of them stayed at our house. Monica was treated just the same as we three girls and "Father Christmas" left her the traditional Christmas Stocking in just the same way.

Mum spoke little of her five brothers and, as they got married, she seemed to have less contact with them. She does tell of the first grandchild to be born and of the brother's reaction. Auntie Aggie, the eldest of Mum's sisters, got married during the First World War to a Canadian soldier. She quickly became pregnant and lived at home until her husband was returned to Canada at the end of the war.

The intrusion of a small, crying baby to an already overcrowded cottage did not fill the five boys with joy. One night, after enduring a night of a crying baby, a chorus came from the attic, "Why don't you drown the little bugger in the piss pot!"

Aggie didn't oblige, but I think the brothers were quite glad when their sister and her offspring went to Canada to live.

CHAPTER
FOUR

My Immediate Family

Vote, vote, vote for Dr. Addison,
Kick old Banksy out the door,
For he's only made of jelly
And we'll kick him in the belly
And he won't come knocking any more.

So went the song we children sang at the approach to a general election in the early 1930s. Looking back on it, I probably had more influence on the outcome of the election through my vociferous advertising campaign than many of the women of the neighbourhood.

"Why won't you vote, Mum?" my sisters asked.

"I leave all that stuff to your father," was Mum's reply. "I don't understand politics. Anyway, I figure whoever gets elected won't do anything for the likes of you and me."

The suffragettes had done sterling work in the early part of the 20th century to further the cause of women towards political emancipation. However, it was probably the women's role in the war years of 1914 to 1918 which did most to win them their right to vote. The year 1924 saw the first woman Member of

Parliament. Yet my mother, like many of her working class contemporaries, still felt that politics was a man's world and never bothered to vote at the time of general or local elections.

Mum and Dad were born and bred in Cirencester, a sleepy Cotswold town. They were both from working class backgrounds and had each lost one parent by the time they were married on 8th August 1919. Their marriage was successful because of their mutual trust and respect. For each birthday or anniversary it was Dad's custom to write a poetic message, in soap, on the mirror over the fireplace in the living room. We all looked forward to these, often amusing, messages but it was not until many years after his death that I really appreciated his skill, wit and literary expertise. Here is an example of his work:

TERESA
Today our married life adds up to 41 long years,
Let's think of all the joy they've brought,
and just forget the tears.
To live in perfect harmony,
and never have heartache,
Just cultivate that quality of simply "give and take".

Mum was a practising Roman Catholic and Dad was a member of the Church of England and a choirboy at the local church. To a certain extent this religious persuasion was part of the reason why their education was different. They both began school life in the local Board School but Dad was given a couple of years of grammar school education by the philanthropic gesture of a titled family in the area. In return for singing at weekday services held in the Manor House, Dad had his education at the grammar school paid for by the Lord of the Manor.

Mum, coming from such a large family, had to leave school as soon as she was able — at thirteen years of age. Yet I always felt Mum was an intelligent person. Had she been given the opportunity I know she would have aspired to a more prestigious career. As it was, she was happy (as were most women of her era) to accept her lot as a housewife and mother.

Their personalities were quite different, partly conditioned by their upbringing, education and quality of life. Dad had an outgoing personality but he was no extrovert. He was friendly with everyone, slow to criticise but shrewd in his judgement of people. He had a great sense of humour and could tell a joke with anyone but he was never crude; indeed he was extremely sober in his language and topics of conversation, at least in the presence of his family — I suspect because we were all female.

Mum always said Dad had a temper if he was roused but I never saw it, although I am sure I must have driven him to distraction at times. Mum says that in all their married life (well over 40 years) she only saw Dad in a temper twice. Once it was with Kath. I believe, as a child, she defied him over something and he lost his temper to such an extent that Mum had to stand between them.

Dad never swore — at least never at home or in front of his family. What happened whilst he was a work I do not know but I suspect that even there his language was far more restrained than many of his factory colleagues. Only once did any of us hear him swear and that was when he was laying new linoleum in the living room. He cut it short and let out a "damn". We were all so shocked that we stopped and gaped open-mouthed at him. He apologized — then we all fell about laughing.

Dad was free of major vices. He was certainly a faithful husband. He did not drink to excess. In fact none of us can remember him ever getting drunk. He liked a drink and visited the Morris Street Working Men's Club every evening to partake of half a pint of beer. That was all he could afford, so that was all he ever had. He smoked a pipe, but again not to excess. He had two ounces of Robin Readbreast tobacco each week and that had to last him. At Christmas or birthday times he would occasionally be given extra tobacco or a cigar on which to over-indulge. Even today, the thing that evokes most good memories in me and epitomizes Christmas festivities is the smell of cigar smoke.

Dad was not a gambling man. To my knowledge he never entered a betting shop. I suspect this was because he never had any spare cash and his family's needs came top of his financial priorities. On one occasion his "mates" at work persuaded him to put a shilling on a horse in the Grand National. He did so. The horse fell at the first fence and broke its neck. His mates said it was because "Geoff Wood's shilling was too heavy for him."

Dad was quite musical. He played the violin and his excellent boy soprano voice, which had gained him access to the church choir, developed into a deep bass. He loved music and, as a boy and young man, took part in local amateur productions of Gilbert and Sullivan operettas. He often gave us renderings of popular songs from these shows. There was no excess fund from the family coffers to allow him to attend concerts but Dad was content with his home-made gramophone and records (the Bakelite 78rpms of the day) which he invariably received as birthday presents. He instilled in us children a love of music by arranging many a pleasant evening of listening to records. Richard Tauber was his favourite tenor but his enjoyment of music was diverse. He had records of Gracie Fields as well as religious songs such as *The Old Rugged Cross* (my Mother's favourite) and *The Lost Chord*.

We would all crowd round the table and search through the wooden box of records to choose the next one to be played.

"Watch where you are putting your elbow, Margaret," was Dad's warning. Too late. I had leaned on one of the records resulting in a loud "crack".

"Oh, dear," was Dad's resigned remark. "I do hope it wasn't my favourite *Eton Boating Song*."

Sure enough, it was. I think I was as devastated as he was sad, and I saved all my pocket money until I could replace it for him as his next birthday present.

When the family moved to Swindon, Dad was invited to join the famous GWR Male Voice Choir. He took a voice test and passed with flying colours.

However, the choir rehearsed on a Sunday afternoon and Dad put his family first and declined the offer. As he worked five and a half days a week, Sunday was the only day he could spend with the family. He was not prepared to relinquish a minute of that precious time.

Dad always put his family first and Mum devoted her whole life to the family.

She was a quiet, unassuming woman but no "push over" if it came to standing up for her family. She worked night and day to provide a good home for us all with never a thought for herself or a moment of complaining. Mum was a gentle, God-fearing woman who always relied upon and supported her husband. If we children wanted anything she usually said, "Ask your father". If decisions about where to go for holidays had to be made, it was a case of "We will wait and see what your father wants to do."

Money was always scarce. Although Mum was the better "manager of money", Dad certainly never handed over the purse strings to her. Indeed, Mum never knew how much Dad earned. She was given as much as he could afford to feed and clothe us all. Dad looked after all the other bills. They managed expertly. I never remember being told "We can't afford it". Between them they saved for holidays and the added expense of Christmas and birthdays.

Just as Dad was handy in the house, making and repairing things, so Mum was expert in the kitchen and with knitting and sewing. She made most of our clothes and taught us all how to knit and sew. Her cooking was plain but wholesome and she was patient enough to allow us to learn, by helping her, at a very early age.

She was kind and considerate to the extent of sometimes being taken for granted. If any member of the extended family was ill, Mum was the first to offer to visit or look after them. Her large family of brothers, sisters, in-laws, nephews and nieces were always made welcome at our house and treated the same as her own family, despite the obvious restricted finance.

Mum had few talents beyond those needed to be a good home-maker. She had not had the opportunity to acquire any skills nor to develop any possible latent talents. She had never attended the theatre or concerts, indeed, I think a trip to the cinema was reserved for adulthood when she was earning her own money. Her hard life in a large, poor family had been her "school of hard knocks". She never complained about her lot in life. Her philosophy was "There's always someone worse off than me". There were times of great hardship — The Depression of the 1920s, the General Strike of 1926 and the Second World War of 1939–1945. During these times Mum went without food and new clothes herself so that we children and her husband would not have to go short.

Mum was a good listener. She was ready to offer advice but never worried if such advice was ignored. One thing I shall always be grateful for is that, after ignoring her advice and making many mistakes in my life, she never once said, "I told you so".

"Now look what you've done," Mum reprimanded Kath and me as Win went to her in tears.

"We didn't touch her," was our chorused reply.

It was true that Kath and I were fighting, as usual. Win was merely the sensitive onlooker. Kath and I were of the same temperament and personality. We were both quite independent and wouldn't let anyone take us for granted. From being a shy child, I developed into an extrovert. We enjoyed life and were relatively relaxed when life dealt us blows. Win was quite the opposite. She was a sensitive child who turned into a nervous adult who worried about everything — her own problems and those of everyone else. I guess that personality-wise, Win took after Mum and Kath and I took after Dad.

In the case of disputes, Kath and I would settle our differences by arguing, shouting and ultimately by coming to blows. Win would not even argue — she preferred to give in and let us have our way.

I always shared a bedroom with Kath. It could not have been easy for her having a sister ten years her junior with her until the day she married. For my part, I couldn't understand why I shouldn't have the small box room to myself. After all, I was the last to arrive. Kath and Win had always shared a bedroom so they were used to each other. It was not until very late in life that Win explained the reason. She was such a nervous child that she couldn't sleep unless she could see the bedroom light from Mum and Dad's room — a feat impossible from the shared back bedroom.

Despite our tendency to fight, Kath was exceedingly good to me. Apparently it was she who gave my parents the £2 needed to ensure Father Christmas could bring me a much demanded doll's pram one Christmas. In later years, when she was courting, I was invited to "Big Band" concerts (including all the current Show Bands such as Glen Miller and his Orchestra). She and her boyfriend, Bill, attended lots of these concerts and were more than willing to take me along despite the 10-year age gap.

Kath and Bill were keen cyclists and the proud owners of a tandem. Many times I was invited out with them for cycle rides. When the journey became too long or arduous, I was allowed on the back of the tandem where I could, to some extent, conserve my energy.

Win played endlessly with me when I was small, especially with my dolls. We spent long hours knitting and sewing dolls' clothes. Win taught me a lot, but games with her were always more sedate. I was a tomboy at heart and needed a sparring partner. I found that in Kath.

It's strange that in our later years, especially after the deaths of our parents, Win and I became really close.

CHAPTER
FIVE

Leisure Time

It is difficult for children of the 21st century to understand how those of the 1930s could enjoy their free time without television or computer games. But my childhood days were full, happy and exciting. Besides the obvious hobbies of stamp collecting, cigarette card collecting and so forth, I read a lot. Despite money being in short supply, Dad bought me a comic each week. At first it was *Tiny Tots* which was a colourful picture comic in which the longer words had been broken down into syllables to aid the young child's attempts to read. Sometimes I got an extra comic — *Beano* or *Dandy* — and later I had the weekly *Film Fun* comic, for which I had to beat my father to the door to lay claim to it before he could get his hands on it! He read it avidly each week.

We listened to the radio quite a lot. It was a family pastime but children were especially interested in the BBC Children's Hour hosted, in the 1930s by "Uncle Mac". Series such as *Toy Town* with characters with comic voices such as Larry the Lamb were listened to with great interest. Uncle Mac used to sign off at the end of the programme with the words:

"Be good, but not so good that someone asks, 'What have you been up to?'."

We enjoyed many outdoor pursuits, not least cycling. I guess I was riding a bicycle by the time I was five years old and, with few motor vehicles on the road, was out unaccompanied by the time I was nine or ten. Groups of children would cycle for miles into the country, often taking picnics and staying out for hours on end. In the spring we picked bluebells in Binal Woods, near Wootton Bassett. In the late summer we went blackberrying. Our stint of blackberrying was followed by a session of jam-making. Mum made sufficient jams to last the family throughout the year and our favourite was blackberry and apple. It took relatively little time for Mum to weigh the ingredients and set it on the gas cooker to simmer. Every time someone passed through the kitchen Mum would call out, "Give my jam a stir!" or "Just test to see if the jam is set."

Setting stage was tested by putting a spoonful of the mixture on a saucer and leaving it for a few minutes to see if it began to set, rather than remain in its liquid state. I guess the whole family had a hand in jam-making and woe betide anyone who let the simmering jam stick to the saucepan!

As I have mentioned, Mum was always knitting and sewing and we organised knitting and sewing parties both in our house and, when the weather permitted, in the back garden. Sometimes the parties were just of children but at other times several mothers attended. We graduated from dolls' clothes to making our own clothes. Fair Isle patterns were mastered at a very early age and we knitted all our own gloves, thick woollen ones for winter and fine lacy patterns of silk or cotton for the summer.

Not all our hobbies were entirely safe. I am sure my parents knew little of some of the activities to which I aspired.

Living close to a railway line, the children in our neighbourhood were avid train spotters. We spent hours waiting for trains to pass over the Bruce Street bridge en route to Gloucester and the Midlands. Sometimes we climbed the bank and put a penny on the line, amazed at the flatness and heat of the metal after the train had passed over it.

Like most towns, neighbourhoods were little communities of like families. Bruce Street, a part of Rodbourne, was a street of relatively new terraced houses which attracted families with young children, not least because of its proximity to the local school, church, chapel and shops and, of course, the main employer, the Great Western Railway.

Friends were in abundance. Neighbouring families inevitably contained at least one child of a similar age to myself and/or my sisters. Within a few houses either side of our house could be counted some ten children all of a similar age. Next door to our family were the Whitings. Their youngest child, Hubert, became a firm friend and constant playmate. Indeed several of the neighbours' children were boys so I became a bit of a tomboy. This delighted my father who had always wanted a son and who was only too pleased to buy me electric train sets, Scaletrix cars, and soldiers and forts for my birthday and Christmas presents.

After school hours and on Saturdays were times to congregate on the field at the back of our houses and in front of the local school, which we all attended. There we built dens, dug holes and lit the odd illicit bonfire.

"Aren't we lucky our 'backsies' have been made up," we often exclaimed.

Loosely translated this meant that we appreciated the fact that the road forming the back entrances to our row of houses was concreted, the opposite side of the street retained the original unmade "dirt" road which inevitably became muddy and water-logged during inclement weather.

Each season of the year had its own principal pastime. There were the marbles season, whips and tops season, and so-on. Each of these games could be enjoyed with the minimum of outlay. Mum and Dad would buy me a small bag of marbles (5 or 10) or I would save my twopence pocket money each week until I could buy my own.

"How about a game of marbles?" a friend would enquire.

"Okay, but no 'keepers'."

I was never very expert at the game so preferred to rely on the scoring of points for each hit rather than the practice of keeping the opponent's marble if a hit was achieved. Besides, some of my friends seemed to have acquired at least one glass marble the size of a golf ball! Eventually I acquired one of these huge marbles myself and naïvely thought it to be indestructible. One day, whilst playing in the street which was relatively safe from traffic, the Co-op Baker's horse and cart came along. This was a common sight and the roundsman was a man with a wooden leg who always had a friendly word for us children. The horse seemed to know all the customers and trundled along the street largely uncontrolled, stopping at the houses of the regular customers. This day we merely stopped our game whilst the horse and cart passed. The cart with its huge steel covered wooden wheels passed over our game and I thought my huge marble would merely be knocked out of the way but . . . the inevitable happened. When the cart had passed by, my pride and joy had been reduced to glass dust by its wheels.

Whips and tops were enjoyed by all of us for a short period. Admittedly one had to buy the top (a small wooden sphere with a metal tip) but the whip could be made out of a stick with string tied to it. The object was to get the top spinning and then "whack it" with the string so that it travelled along the road whilst rotating.

"Mum, I need a whip for my top," I pleaded.

"Find me a stick and I'll make you one."

How was it my mother always had time to stop what she was doing to arcede to my requests? A few minutes perusing the contents of Dad's shed produced a straight stick and some old string. In no time at all I had the right equipment.

"Mum, I can't get my top started."

With the briefest of sighs, Mum put down the vegetable knife and came with me to the "backsies" to show me how to wind the string of the whip tightly

42

round the top and then release it with a sharp pull. Other parents taught their children how to start a top with a quick hand rotation. Parents' time spent on instructions proved to be well spent for we amused ourselves every waking moment for days on end, until the next craze came into season.

Hopscotch and skipping were two games which seemed to last throughout the year and involve the whole neighbourhood. I remember large chalked squares appearing on pavements and children waiting patiently for their turns to hop from one to the other, picking up the stone, which was the object of the game.

Skipping was something every child mastered, all of the girls and most of the boys. We were taught how to skip at school. A few had the proper skipping ropes with handles, some of which had bells inside them, but we all managed a piece of rope. I hate to think how many washing lines mysteriously disappeared during skipping seasons!

In an afternoon or summer evening it was not uncommon for the mums to join us kids in the street. A long length of rope spanning the road would be turned by a couple of mums and we would all join in the skipping. Mums would insist on having their turns at skipping. Why should they just be the rope turners? Jolting breasts and flabby stomachs were ignored as we all joined in the fun.

I was very fortunate in having a father who was what today would be called a "DIY fanatic". Dad's endeavours at building, decorating and generally making anything for the home or family was born out of necessity. Money was tight. If Father Christmas was to bring us the much-demanded dolls' house, dolls' cot, toy shop etc, he needed a helping hand. Dad spent hours of his free time in his shed until the masterpiece was ready for Mum to provide the finishing touches — curtains and knitted rugs for the dolls' house, bedding and dolls' clothes for the cot or pram.

"Can I have a pair of stilts, Mum?"

Yes, a new play season was upon us — stilt walking.

"Ask your father when he comes home for dinner," was the reply.

By 12.30p.m., when the factory hooter blew to announce the beginning of lunch break, I was at the garden gate waiting for Dad's return. Precisely ten minutes later he appeared round the corner, having walked home with one of his "mates" and a neighbour.

"Can I have some stilts, Dad? Mum said I had to ask you."

"Not just at this minute. I've got half an hour to eat my dinner. I'll see what I can do on Saturday."

Sure enough, by Saturday a beautiful pair of dual height wooden stilts had been lovingly constructed by my Dad in his beloved shed!

For Dad, it was not sufficient to tack two lumps of wood to the side of poles as most of my friends had managed. My stilts had rounded poles of silky smooth wood with foot rests on either side so that I had "adjustable" heights. On one side the foot rests were some six to eight inches from the floor so that I could practise the art without undue distress. On the other side of the poles the foot rests were some two to three feet from the ground. Only an expert could manage stilt walking to this degree! Not content with making the stilts, Dad came out into our "backsies" and showed me and my friends the art of stilt walking. My friends were so envious of me but I just brushed it off with the common assumption, "Oh, my Dad can make anything."

Roller skating was another pastime which survived throughout the year. Almost every child learned to skate. Pairs of skates were acquired as birthday or Christmas presents. Ball-bearing skates were the fastest and those who possessed them aspired to "professional" status in their tricks and speed. Not only were we fortunate at having a concrete back road to our houses on which to skate but, at the end of the street, there were a few shops in front of which was a large paved area. That, to me, became my stage. For years I dreamed of becoming a professional skater and performing on stage. That was some half a century before the emergence of "Starlight Express" on the West End stage!

Later, my prowess at roller-skating led to the teenage pastime of spending time at the local roller skating rink.

Mum was not house-proud. Our house was always clean and relatively tidy but it was a home first and foremost. If it was a wet holiday I was always allowed to have friends in to play. Unless the weather was very cold we would play under the verandah — another example of Dad's handiwork. Often there were six or seven of us playing there. If we were playing "houses", we purloined many of Mum's kitchen utensils until a plea came from the kitchen, "Do you think I could have a couple of saucepans back so that I can get your father's dinner on?"

Inside the house we were allowed to get all sorts of toys out in the living room. I remember a big tin of bricks, not wooden ones but actual hard bricks similar to the real thing. We built all manner of things with these. Who needed a toy fort, shop, dolls' house, when we could make our own out of bricks?

We turned the living room into a schoolroom and littered the table with paper, pens, crayons and paints. We moved the furniture around to resemble a hospital ward and played doctors and nurses; the living room became a shop, a house, a battlefield, according to our imaginations and the number of friends involved. By twelve o'clock everything had to be cleared away so that Mum could lay the table for dinner which had to be on the table at 12.40p.m. precisely so that Dad could enjoy his lunch in peace before leaving for work again at 1.20p.m.

The weekends were a family time. Dad worked until 12.30p.m. on Saturdays but Saturday afternoons and Sundays were family times. Dad often went to Cirencester to visit his elderly Mum on Saturday afternoon, leaving Mum to take us three children into town for some "window shopping". There was seldom money to spend on buying anything but we enjoyed just looking!

Sunday was devoted to Mass in the morning — a two-mile walk each way to the nearest Catholic church — followed by a roast lunch and a "rest" in the afternoon. How I hated the ridiculous idea of having to go to bed during the day! But the reward was to be allowed to stay up late in the evening.

In the summer we went for long walks on a Sunday evening, usually across fields. We walked through Rodbourne Cheney and across the fields to Stratton (now part of Penhill) or to Moredon or Haydon Wick. For children, walks of some five to ten miles must have been quite arduous but we were encouraged to stop and pick flowers on the way. That was more enjoyable than the insistence that, on return, they had to be sorted and put into water. Even wild flowers were treated with respect and, once picked, must not be left to die.

Occasionally we would venture out on bicycles, which we all had, but Mum was not a good cyclist so that pastime was usually left to Dad who accompanied us children until we were old enough to venture out alone.

During winter evenings a fire was lit in the front room and we gathered there to play family board games such as Ludo, Snakes and Ladders, Sorry, or card games such as Happy Families. We also had other games such as Bagatelle. We children were schooled into being good sports by not being allowed to cheat and certainly never allowed to win unless justly so.

"If you are going to whine and grizzle, you can stop playing."

I was having particularly bad luck at Bagatelle and showed my impatience and displeasure. I sat sulking, watching enviously as the rest of the family competed.

"I just need a 10 to win," said Mum.

"I'll get it for you if you let me have a go," I offered. It took many such pleas on my part and several unsuccessful attempts on my mother's part before she said. "Oh, all right, Big Head, you get me a 10."

I pulled back the spring, the metal ball shot out, up to the top of the board, and lodged neatly into the 10 slot. Everyone fell about laughing. I guess I was too young to understand why they all laughed or to appreciate why I was not congratulated on my expertise!

THE CHILDREN'S FETE

A much-anticipated annual event was the Children's Fête held in the Park by St. Mark's Church (a part of the Swindon Railway Village provided by the GWR). The park was turned into a massive fairground. Each railway worker's child had a free ticket of admission which entitled them to a free fruit cake and two free rides. Other rides cost a few pence each so we eagerly saved pocket money to spend at this event.

"Dad, I've dropped my shilling down this hole."

I had been standing at the back window patiently waiting for the rest of the family to get ready to leave for the fete. My shilling was the result of saving pocket money for several weeks and would provide some five or six rides at the fair. Now it was gone, slipped down between the wooden window-sill and the back wall of the room.

"Never mind," said Dad. "I'll see if I can get it out."

Within minutes, working from the outer wall, he had chipped away at the mortar between the bricks, carefully lifted out two bricks at what he thought would be the point to which it had dropped and retrieved the shilling. The re-cementing of the bricks could wait until a less demanding time!

There was always a central spectacle at the Fête — fire-eaters, stilt walkers, clowns, acrobats, stunt motor cyclists, tight ropewalkers . . . One year we watched the famous Houdini.

"Let's go now," suggested Win.

It must have been about six o'clock. The Fête ended with a spectacular firework display of which Win was terrified. The thought of this meant that either Win pleaded with us to go home from late afternoon onwards or we all returned home for tea about five o'clock and then Dad, Kath and I returned early evening for the fireworks.

During the afternoon, Kath and I would try all the most exciting rides whilst Win restricted her enjoyment to a ride on the round horses. Kath and I loved anything that was fast but I was never allowed on the chair-o'- planes and bumper cars. Kath being ten years older than me got to ride on almost anything she liked. But whatever excitement the rides held, nothing compared with the fireworks.

Kath and I revelled in the loudest bangers and jumping crackers. If Win had been persuaded to stay until dusk she now either clasped her hands over her ears or tugged at Mum in an attempt to drag her from the park. The final spectacle was always a tableau depicting some famous person or event.

Perhaps, if we had been allowed our own fireworks for Guy Fawkes Night, Win would have got used to them, but Dad always insisted that to buy fireworks was like burning money. We were lucky to get a sixpenny bag of sparklers!

CHAPTER
SIX

Holidays

Annual paid holidays were so unique to the employees of GWR in Swindon that I have devoted a chapter to this phenomenon.

In the early 20th century, workers had fought hard, through their Trade Unions, to achieve an eight-hour day but it took a much longer fight to achieve paid annual holidays for all. In common with some other employers across the country, the GWR closed for one week in July to give all the workers an annual holiday. At first this was unpaid and many referred to it as a "lock-out". It must have been hard to budget, from a meagre wage, for a week with no pay let alone save to enjoy trips out of town during that week.

Mum and Dad always ensured we went to the seaside for that week which was known as "Trip Week" in Swindon. Mum saved her "Co-op Divi", the half-yearly monetary reward for shopping at the local Co-operative Society. We always had "rooms and attendance" at the resort, which meant Mum and Dad got the use of two bedrooms and a sitting room in a private house. The owner (the landlady) cooked meals for us from food Mum provided.

This was the cheapest form of lodgings. Mum paid around five shillings for each room for the week so for under a pound we had somewhere to eat and sleep, and Mum didn't have to cook or do housework. Mum reckoned that we had to eat if we stayed at home, so the cost of our food was not a consideration. We ate plain, wholesome food, just as we did at home. There was little money for "treats" but Dad would usually find enough for us children to have an ice cream each day. At what time of the day we consumed this ice cream was our decision. We knew that if we chose to have it whilst playing on the sands during the day, there would be no ice cream whilst we were out for our evening walk.

Dad saved up throughout the year so that he had enough pocket money for such treats. We normally got at least one trip out to sea, often in a hired rowing boat which Dad rowed quite expertly. Occasionally there was a trip on a paddle steamer.

I recall one such trip whilst we were staying in Weymouth. Dad hired a rowing boat and took me and a friend, Heather May, out on the sea in it. I guess we children were about seven years old at the time. The water was calm and the weather sunny and warm. As usual we children were thrilled and begged Dad to go farther and farther out to sea.

Suddenly large waves started to gather and the boat rolled and tossed quite alarmingly. Another man was close by with his children, obviously on a similar trip.

"What do you suggest we do?" he shouted to Dad, although why he should have thought Dad had any better idea than he did, was beyond us. I was not unduly worried. I liked a little excitement and a small boat tossed by huge waves certainly provided excitement. Anyway, Dad always knew what to do so I had complete confidence in our safety.

"I reckon we should hit the waves broadside on," this man continued without waiting for Dad to reply to his question.

"Don't be a fool, man, that would just flip the boat over." I knew Dad would have the answer. "Just point the nose to the shore and keep rowing."

Both men did just that. Heather and I were in our elements. Dad must have been a little nervous but he treated it all as a huge joke. The other man was less controlled and showed signs of sheer fright which he was having difficulty concealing from his two frightened passengers. We called out to the other children and laughed and joked with them until they, also, found the whole episode very enjoyable.

Mum was unable to see the funny side of the escapade when we reached the beach.

"What made you take those children out in such seas?" she ranted. "Don't you realise you could all have been drowned?"

"But . . . but . . ." Dad tried to explain but it was no use. Mum cradled us in her arms and dried our splashed faces, unable to understand that we had had the most exciting ride of our short lives.

It transpired that there were some warships out at sea, quite close to Portland Harbour which had been on manoeuvres and they were responsible for the huge waves which invaded Weymouth Bay.

Sometimes, depending on the resort, Dad would buy a bag of crabs' claws from the local fishmonger's on the way to the beach. He would crack them open between two large pebbles and we would sit and pick out and eat the flesh. Dad used his penknife but the rest of us used hairpins or hair slides. The delicacy was much appreciated since we could never afford to eat the crabs or lobsters for which the resort was famous.

Each day was the same — down to the beach after breakfast and stay there until tea-time. Then, after our early evening meal, a walk, usually along the promenade. I cannot recall my early "Trip" holidays but, apart from the war years, I know we always went to the seaside for a week — later for two weeks.

"Trip" holiday was always the first week of July. By the late 1930s the GWR relented and gave all its workers full pay for that week. Eventually the one week was extended to two weeks and my parents duly saved enough for us to enjoy two weeks at the seaside.

One of the privileges of working for the GWR was cheap travel. Employees and their families could apply for as many "cheap" rail tickets (one-third off the normal fare) as they wanted but once a year they were granted a "free pass" for the whole family. Naturally most families used their free passes to go on the "Trip" holiday. The company laid on special trains to the popular destinations and families flocked to the station to join their designated trains. There were so many trains that some had to leave from the "sidings" near the engine sheds. Getting aboard trains which were not at the station platform provided some hilarious situations.

"Give her a shove up the backside," was a common piece of advice from the waiting passengers when some rather plump lady found negotiating a short step-ladder rather daunting.

Departure times were staggered so that those leaving for distant destinations, like Cornwall or Scotland, left late on Friday evening and travelled through the night. We often took our holiday in St. Ives, Cornwall. Our special train left about 11p.m on Friday and we arrived in St. Ives about 5a.m. on Saturday. Naturally we children slept for most of the journey, after the initial excitement of the day and holiday prospects had subsided.

I remember such journeys vividly.

"Margaret, wake up, wake up."

Mum's gentle shaking roused me, not very willingly, from my sleep.

"We're just coming up to Saltash Bridge."

That was something not to be missed. Loyal to their employer's heritage, GWR employees were in awe of Isambard Kingdom Brunel's great steel bridge spanning the River Tamar just outside Plymouth. If one leaned out of the train window as the bridge was approached, one could see the front of the train with its puffing engine billowing white steam as it passed under the portico of the bridge. Then followed the thrill of being conveyed high above the water to cross this wide river. The sight was so memorable that we were all prepared for the smuts of coal dust which inevitably got in our eyes as we hung our heads from the windows and looked towards the coal-eating engine which was pulling our train.

"Wow, isn't it big."

"How on earth did they build it so high up, and over water?"

Our questions were eagerly answered by parents who knew all about the founder of "God's Wonderful Railway" and his achievements.

"I've got something in my eye," I wailed as some hot ash pricked my eye and my lid shut tight over watering eye sockets.

"You should know you have to squint," was the only sympathy I got from Mum.

"Let's have a look," suggested Dad. He was a genius at getting things out of eyes. He had trained with the St. John Ambulance Brigade and was often called upon to get bits of steel shavings out of the eyes of fellow workers. A speck of coal dust was a simple task for him, even if it was from a scared child. A second or two later the offending speck was removed and my head was, once again, thrust out of the carriage window, inviting a repeat of the operation.

Such was the influence of the GWR, being the main employers in the town, that Swindon became a ghost town over this period. For those unable to afford to go away for a holiday, the Wednesday of "Trip Week" was a day when extra trains were laid on to take families on day trips to the coast. That day Swindon was "dead". Most shops closed. It resembled a Sunday.

Because whole train-loads of GWR workers from the Swindon works descended upon the popular south coast resorts, being on holiday was more like home from home. Almost all the families stayed in private houses, either on bed and breakfast terms or rooms and attendance, as we did. The landladies looked forward to their guests returning year after year and, despite, the early arrival of our special trains, were always at the station ready to greet their guests. Should this be your first visit it was likely that the landlady would be on the platform calling out the name of your family so that she could identify her guests and escort them to their temporary home.

We travelled relatively lightly. Trunks containing all our holiday clothes were sent ahead, free of charge, by the GWR so by the time we got to our destination we merely had to unpack. I well remember Mum spending days the week prior to the holiday getting all our clothes washed and ironed, rationing what we could have to wear for the last couple of days before the holiday when most of our clothes were already in transit. I remember I always insisted on my swimming costume being kept back and going in the one small case we took as hand luggage.

"What if the trunk doesn't arrive before us, or gets lost?" I would query. "How long would I have to wait before I could go swimming? I want to go in the sea every single day so I need my costume with me all the time."

Mum pandered to my fears and refrained from putting my swimming costume in the trunk which, incidentally, was never late arriving and never got lost in transit!

One year, when we went to Weymouth for our Trip holiday, the demand for extra trains meant that, by the time coaches were allocated to the somewhat shorter journeys (including Weymouth), there were no corridor trains available. I guess the journey was only about three hours but this could prove a problem when there were no toilet facilities "along the corridor".

By the time we reached Castle Cary, Dad was desperate to go to the toilet. The train came to a halt and Dad stuck his head out of the window.

"How long do we stay here?" he enquired of a porter on the platform. "Time for me to go to the toilet?"

"Sorry, mate," came the reply, "we've only stopped for a signal. We'll probably be off in a couple of minutes. The toilet is on another platform, over the bridge."

Dad turned to his family.

"Sorry, folks, I've just got to go. See you in Weymouth . . . sometime."

With that he left the train and progressed at a quick pace along the platform and over the bridge. Sure enough the stop was very brief. The train pulled out of the station before Dad had even found the toilet.

We were not unduly perplexed by Dad's absence until we arrived in Weymouth when Mum realized we were all travelling on one ticket, Dad's free pass, so there was no way we could leave the station until we were reunited with him. I guess it was about half an hour later when a short, local train pulled into the station and out stepped Dad.

"Sorry I had to leave you like that but it was a case of necessity. As it was the next train was a local 'stopper' with very few passengers so I had a very pleasant journey. Now, let's get out of here and find the sea."

As I've said, many popular seaside resorts were "invaded" by the Swindon GWR workers' families during the first two weeks of July. Many friendships were made with locals and resulted in some good-humoured rivalry. There were water polo matches in the sea with competing teams being drawn from the locals and from Swindon holidaymakers. Cricket matches, formal and informal were played on the beach. Of course families joined together for all sorts of ball games, sandcastle building and races.

On a visit to St. Ives in Cornwall there was a competition to see who could swim from one side of Porthminster Bay to the other. Dad was a good swimmer. His favourite stroke was the single over-arm crawl. He would settle down with his head turned just to one side and his long arm plummeting over his head and into the water. This relaxed stroke gave the impression that he could swim for ever.

"Just going for a dip. Won't be long. Got to get in some practice for the cross the bay swim tomorrow."

With this nonchalant explanation, Dad was off down to the water's edge. With a swift run into the icy water and a plunge straight into his single over-arm crawl, he was off for an enjoyable swim. But it turned out to be anything but an enjoyable experience.

Dad explained, afterwards, that he was enjoying the swim and began to think he was probably nearing the other side of the bay so he raised his head and looked straight ahead. All he could see was the vast Atlantic Ocean. There were no rocks to signal the approach of the other side of the bay. He flipped onto his back and looked around. To his horror, he realized that the current had not taken him across the bay but directly out to sea. The people on the beach were mere specks. He admitted it would have been easy to panic but, typically for Dad, he rested, floating on his back, while he worked out what had to be done. He had to swim for shore but needed to do so leisurely, resting on his back now and again to conserve the little energy he had left. Above all he knew he had to keep focused on the route and his destination — the safety of the beach.

As he approached the shoreline, he could see rows of people calling to him and waving as they had done whilst he, quite obliviously, swam directly out to sea. He arrived back safely, albeit very tired, to be confronted by a frantic wife who let forth with a tirade.

"What on earth were you thinking of? Remember you have a wife and children. Don't ever embark on such a foolhardy swim again. We've all been out of our minds with worry. Didn't you hear us shouting at you to come back?"

Dad was too tired to argue but eventually managed to explain his trip had been somewhat unintentional. Needless to say, Dad was one of the few who eventually competed successfully with the locals in the race from one side of Porthminster Bay to the other.

Mum and Dad always hired a tent or beach hut for the whole holiday. We spent all day on the beach so needed somewhere to change into swimming costumes, to shelter from inclement weather, and to prepare sandwiches for our mid-day meal. Mum usually bought bread rolls, buns and milk on her way to the beach. Tea, a kettle and a primus stove could be left in the beach hut.

"Looks like rain, I'm afraid," Dad announced. The cricket match taking place on the beach was abandoned and everyone returned to their tents and hurriedly took deck chairs, towels and other beach paraphernalia inside.

A clap of thunder heralded the start of a storm which could only be described as a cloud burst. Before long the promenade behind us was flooded as the storm drains could not accommodate the rain. Surface water cascaded on to the already water-logged beach. The Swindonians rallied round. The men and older children went outside the tents armed with spades to dig gullies to keep out the excess water and, hopefully, channel it down to the sea.

"What's she crying for?" Dad enquired of Mum who was sitting in a deck chair with me on her lap.

"I guess she's frightened," Mum explained.

"Are you OK?" Dad enquired of Mum.

"Apart from the fact that I'm sitting in a pool of water, nursing a child who is endeavouring to add to the excess water with her tears . . . I'm fine!"

I have so many happy memories of my Trip holidays. As we left for home each year on our special trains, we would all hang out of the carriage windows and wave at the last vestige of coastline shouting, "Goodbye, sea. See you again next year."

Apart from the war years, we always did just that. It might not have been to the same resort but it would certainly be two weeks' holiday at the seaside.

PART TWO

THE WAR YEARS

CHAPTER
SEVEN

Change of School

There were so many changes in state education during the 20th century that the system in operation at the end of the century bore little resemblance to that in place at the beginning.

When my parents first attended school, it was not free. Their mothers paid a penny a week for each child. Many children left school when they were 11 years old. By the end of the century there was free, compulsory education for all children aged 5–16 years with many children enjoying free education until the age of 18.

When my eldest sister took the grammar school test, she was examined in several subjects and there were two papers and an interview. Free grammar school education was offered to those who passed all sections and a semi-free education to those who passed only part of the examination. My eldest sister fell into this category. Sadly my father was not able to afford the requirement that he buy all books and stationery, so she missed out on a grammar school education. By the end of the century selection at 11 had disappeared in most areas of England.

By the 1930s, Elementary schools provided education for pupils from 4+ to the day they left at 14 years, apart from those who were selected for grammar schools following success in the grammar school test. By the end of the century there were still a few grammar schools left in the state system but most education authorities provided primary education in schools for children 4+ to 11+ and then comprehensive schools for their secondary education, which lasted at least until 16 years.

There were few, if any, church schools in the state system at the beginning of the century but then the Roman Catholic church began to develop its own schools, funded partly by the state and partly by the church. By the end of the century other religious schools were being set up, some funded partly by the state.

"How would you like to change to another school?"

My sister put this question to me whilst we were out on one of the family's Sunday evening walks.

"Why?" I queried.

The local Even Swindon school had been good enough for both Kath and Win, and I had followed in their footsteps as a matter of course. All the children in the neighbourhood where we lived went to Even Swindon School where, unless they passed the grammar school test and transferred to a grammar school, they remained until they left for work at the age of 14 years.

"Well, it's like this," Win began to explain, "You know Mum and Dad have not been going to church much recently and Kath and I have been going to St. Mark's rather than Holy Rood."

"Yes," I replied, wondering what on earth church had to do with school.

"Well, Canon Noonan, the parish priest at Holy Rood, explained that Mum and Dad are excommunicated because they won't send you to Holy Rood School. Dad doesn't mind going to a Church of England church and even told the Canon that he will have Kath and me confirmed at St Mark's, but Mum says 'once a Catholic, always a Catholic'. She wants to stay with the Catholic church and be a full member once again. If you were to go to school at Holy Rood, it would overcome the problem."

"But I'd not have any friends there," I complained.

"You wouldn't have the same school friends as you have now but you would make lots of new ones and you would still have your old friends to play with after school and in the holidays," Win explained.

As a reasonably intelligent nine year old, it didn't take me long to weigh up the situation and, bearing in mind I would be doing my parents a favour as well, I agreed to change to Holy Rood RC School in Groundwell Road — some two miles from home.

The journey to and from school would be made by bus and, with a two-hour lunch break, I would be allowed to come home for my lunch. Thus, in the autumn term of 1939 I began as a pupil of Holy Rood RC School. Little did I appreciate, at the time, what a change this would make to my life.

Holy Rood School buildings dated from the mid-19th century. It was staffed by nuns supplemented by lay staff. Like all state schools, it was an elementary school which catered for children from 4+ years until leaving age at 14 years. In common with other state schools, pupils were entered for the grammar school test and, if successful, transferred to one of the three non-Catholic grammar schools.

Because the parish priest wanted to swell the numbers attending his church school he expected staff to teach very large classes. There were insufficient pupils, staff or classrooms to have a separate teacher for each class, hence each teacher was in charge of one classroom which housed two different age-groups. They were staffed as follows:

Infant Department

Miss Chedzey was in charge of the first two classes, covering children aged between 4 and 5+. In an interview with this lady when she was in her late eighties I got a vivid picture of the influence of the church on the school during its early days. She told me that, at times, her "double class" consisted of up to 70 children.

A nun, Sister Raphael, was in charge of the other two infant classes, which catered for children up to seven years of age. She was a jolly person and well-equipped to teach children of this age. In addition she prepared all children for their First Communion since this was made at 7 years. Being a late comer to the school, I used to go to her class for some religious instruction lessons prior to making my own First Communion when I was nine. I liked Sister Raphael. She was kind, amusing and a very devout Catholic. This laid a good foundation for my own Catholic faith.

Juniors

Sister Andreas had charge of Standards 1 and 2 — children from 7–9 years of age

Sister Andreas was a quiet lady of slight build. Besides her own classes she taught girls Physical Education throughout the school. Pictures of her running around the playground in her long, flowing, black habit are still vivid in my mind. She was in charge of the school's netball team and took us all over the town to play in matches against other schools and to attend netball tournaments. Later she even taught us hockey on the ever-muddy Walcot playing fields.

Mr Rogers taught Standards 3 and 4 in a large classroom which had only three small windows set just below the ceiling, so there was no chance of children being distracted!

Sister Concepta taught Standard 5 which was the "scholarship" class. She was my favourite teacher. She was a large lady who, in her long, black habit, produced a formidable image. She had a quick temper but also a sense of humour. One day, after doing playground duty, she returned to the classroom with bird droppings on her veil. Whilst endeavouring to remove this stain with

69

wet paper, she remarked to the class as a whole, "Isn't it a good job cows don't fly."

Seniors

(for those not able to transfer to the grammar school)

Mr Corrigan taught Standards 6 and 7. He was a quietly spoken, good looking young man adored by his pupils, not least the girls. On reflection he had a wealth of knowledge for not only did he teach us all the compulsory subjects of the school's limited time-table, but he taught boys Physical Education and introduced subjects as diverse as hygiene and gardening to our dull curriculum.

Mr Scanlon was the Headteacher. He was a jolly, family man whose own children attended the school until they passed the grammar school test. He had his own room at the end of the corridor known as "The Desk", to which recalcitrant pupils were sent by their class teacher to receive due punishment for their indiscipline — usually the cane.

As in all schools, the teachers varied in personality and classroom management but all enforced the very strict code of discipline laid down by the Headmaster in conjunction with the parish priest.

Being 9 years old when I started at the school, I was put straight into Mr. Rogers's class — Standard 4. "Scuffer" Rogers, as he was known, was thought by all pupils to be the worst teacher in the whole world, never mind in the school! My classmates commiserated with me at having to go into his class but were envious of the fact that I would only spend one year there whilst they had to endure both years with him.

I must admit "Scuffer" was the grumpiest, least-approachable teacher I have ever met. He had a gruff voice and would bellow at one for the smallest of misdemeanours. Added to this, his lessons were dull, boring, and uninspiring.

The time-table of lessons was equally uninspiring. Each morning consisted of religious instruction and arithmetic. Each afternoon started with English, followed by geography, history, or occasionally physical education, singing (usually hymns) or needlework (for the girls).

In the arithmetic lessons, the times tables were learned by rote. Most mornings the arithmetic lesson started with the chanting of the times tables. This was usually followed by quick-fire mental arithmetic questions. It took all of one's concentration to keep alert to the fact that the next question might be yours, and an inability to give the correct answer might be followed by a piece of flying chalk propelled from the hand of a now frustrated teacher. Arithmetic lessons held no fear for me. I had learned most of my times tables at Even Swindon school, although now we were expected to learn 13- and 14-times tables. I was never a really shy person, so having to answer questions in class was not a problem.

Even at this early age I had developed a love for poetry. To hear beautiful poems droned in the gruff voice of "Scuffer" was sufficient to put any child off poetry for life. Not me. Occasionally, probably when he had been too tired to prepare a proper lesson, he would select a pupil to go and stand at the back of the class and recite a poem of his/her choice, or possibly one which the class had just studied and learnt by rote. I was in my element. I took care to project my voice sufficiently for the words to be heard by all in this huge classroom, not least "Scuffer" who, unless kept awake by a well delivered verse, might just show his complete boredom with his chosen profession by "nodding off".

It was at this time of my life that I really decided on a career in the theatre. To improve my voice and to satisfy my love of poetry my parents agreed to my having private elocution lessons, which I loved.

One afternoon, soon after I had started at Holy Rood School, I found myself with severe stomach ache, which could have probably been relieved by a visit to the toilet. However, the school toilets (situated in an outdoor block which was only partially roofed and nicknamed "The Dubs") was an area I had no intention of using. However much I needed to go to the toilet, I waited until I got home. "The Dubs" smelt awful, there was often no toilet paper, and the flushes seldom worked. If it was raining one had to wait in the unroofed section for a free cubicle.

"Please, sir, I don't feel well."

It took a lot of courage to approach "Scuffer" Rogers but the thought of "The Dubs" was enough to overcome my fear.

"What's wrong?" His reply was surprisingly sympathetic.

"I've got terrible pains in my stomach. I had them when I was at my last school," I lied, "And then they would let me go home. Can I go home now, sir, please?"

To my surprise "Scuffer" agreed and within half an hour I had caught the bus and was walking in through the back door, to the surprise of Mum and Auntie Dink, who was staying with us on holiday.

"What on earth are you doing, coming home at this time?" Mum enquired.

A quick explanation of the need to visit the toilet was followed by a dash to the lavatory and a cure for my pains! On rejoining Mum and Auntie, I explained that I just needed to go to the toilet but that the school toilets were so disgusting I couldn't go there.

"Why didn't you use some of your bus money to visit one of the public toilets in the town?" enquired Mum.

"What, and have to walk home?" I said in disbelief at the idea of a two-mile walk.

Auntie Dink, always one to right a wrong, had the answer.

"Look, my girl, always keep an extra penny in your pocket and next time you want to go to the toilet during school hours, just tell the teacher you are going out of school to visit the public toilets in the town. If he dares to forbid it, just tell him you are not going to use the disgusting toilets they provide; then walk out of the school. Your mother will always back your actions and take delight in revealing the state of the school toilets."

Fortunately I never needed to take Auntie Dink's advice. For the rest of my school days I managed to curtail my toilet visits to times when I was at home.

Being a church school, every morning began with prayers, which were said in the classroom since there was no hall or room large enough to hold a school assembly. Prayers in the nuns' classes tended to be a little longer than those of the lay teachers! The first hour's lesson was always religious instruction, the basis of which, especially in Standards 1–4, was the learning of the Catechism. Questions and answers were learnt by rote. Lay teachers, unable to explain adequately some of the mysteries of this somewhat complex religion, would merely explain that this was something too difficult for humans to comprehend so we must accept it as a matter of faith.

Monday mornings began with the taking of a Mass register. As the attendance at Sunday Mass was compulsory under pain of mortal sin, it was felt essential to check that all children had attended Sunday Mass the previous day. In addition to answering "Mass, sir," we were expected to add "and Catechism" if we had returned in the afternoon for formal religious instruction given, in the school, by the priest.

By the time we reached Standard 5, Sister Concepta's class, Canon Noonan usually attended the religious instruction lesson on a Monday morning and his first task was to inspect the Mass register.

I should explain here that Canon Noonan was a very devout priest. His high moral standards and strict adherence to church law, as well as God's, made him intolerant to the difficulties encountered by Catholics struggling to maintain their faith in a growing secular

74

environment. Naturally his strict code was brought into the classroom each Monday.

On close inspection of the Mass register, those who had not attended Mass were made to stand out in the front of the class whilst the Canon chided them, pointing out what terrible sinners they were and, quite frequently, cuffing them across the head whilst delivering his tirade. I never missed Mass. Despite a two-mile walk from home to church, Mum and Dad made sure we always went to 9.30 a.m. Mass on a Sunday. I usually returned for Catechism in the afternoon but occasionally found myself in front of the class for the lesser misdemeanour of non-attendance at Catechism class. As I grew up I wondered why it never occurred to any of us to tell a "white lie" and say we had been to Mass when, in fact, we hadn't. I guess we were so innocent and so conditioned in the fear of sin that we were sure that Canon Noonan or Sister Concepta would just know we were lying.

The religious instruction lesson lasted until the mid-morning break of about 20 minutes during which we were turned out into the playground. The two playgrounds (one for the girls and one for the boys, divided by a high wall) were quite inadequate for the number of children in the school. The girls' playground was bounded by the main Groundwell Road so there were always people and traffic to watch since the space for playing games was very restricted. To reach the girls' cloakroom, one had to leave by the main entrance and go around the playground and in by another door. On cold days there was a mad rush through the wind and rain to get one's coat, or better still to linger in the warm cloakroom until the teacher on duty turned us out.

The second morning lesson was always arithmetic and the afternoon sessions began with English — my favourite subject, even though much time was taken up by handwriting practice and learning to spell by rote. Every desk was equipped with a dictionary which we were expected to use to excess.

After a year at Holy Rood School, I progressed to Sister Concepta's class and began a year of preparation for the dreaded grammar school test.

"Instead of doing written work today, I'm going to tell you a story."

To our delight, Sister Concepta seemed to be in a good mood and, although we 10 year olds felt that listening to stories was a little beneath us, intellectually, the thought of this activity was infinitely better than spelling tests, composition or handwriting practice.

The story concerned a Scottish nobleman called Macbeth. It was an exciting story in which Macbeth's wife helped him to successfully murder King Duncan so that he could become King. The scheming, plotting and eventual murder of Duncan, Macbeth's accession to the throne and his own eventual demise kept us spellbound.

Throughout the year, Sister Concepta repeated this "story time", introducing us to other tragic characters such as Hamlet and King Lear, and to comic characters such as Malvolio and Sir Toby Belch. Not once was the name Shakespeare mentioned. Some years later I recognised these as Shakespeare's plays but, by then, I was "hooked". My love of poetry and my awakening interest in the characters and plots caused me to become a devoted student of Shakespeare and a life-long admirer of "The Bard".

Religious instruction lessons in Sister Concepta's class were boring. We were now considered adult enough to have learnt our Catechism and to be able to study church history. This subject was contained in a book so boring that I took an instant dislike to the subject. The textbook had very small print, long words, a florid style and there were no pictures. We read the book with little interest and no retention of the facts contained therein.

At this age, boys were encouraged to become altar servers and thus had to learn the responses to the Latin Mass. Their training was inflicted upon the whole class. We chanted these responses in class and listened to them during Mass. Until I got a Sunday Missal as a birthday present and could read the English translation, I was ignorant of what was being said.

One of the delights of being in Sister Concepta's class was the actual classroom layout. Holy Rood School had one main corridor running from front to back of the building with classrooms on either side. On one side there was a large hall which was divided off into three classrooms by screens. These were for the two infant classes and Mr Rogers' Standards 3 and 4. I often wondered why Sister Andreas's Standards 1 and 2 were not accommodated in that last room since it was a natural age progression for the students, but I guess it was the prerogative of the nuns to demand the more pleasant rooms.

On the other side of the corridor there were three classrooms with windows on the playground side and curtained windows on the corridor side. The floors of these three rooms were "stepped" to form three distinct tiers. Whilst most pupils liked to sit at the back of the class, as far away from the teacher as possible, it had to be appreciated that the back row was, perhaps, even more visible and the middle tier was largely at eye level for the teacher.

We sat in strict rows of double desks consisting of a flat working surface and a lift up double seat. How I longed for a desk to myself — with a lid!

THE GRAMMAR SCHOOL TEST

By the time I had to take this examination, in the Spring term of 1941, it consisted of just two tests — arithmetic and English. However, there were still two parts to the examination, taken at separate times. Those who were successful in the first examination were allowed to sit the second.

So demanding was this examination that some 80 per cent of candidates failed to gain grammar school places each year. Looking back on this time I realise the tremendous pressure put upon most children. Their future education and, ultimately, their destiny in regards to their working life was governed by their success or failure at this examination. Some parents had their children coached for the examination; others made extravagant promises, for instance a new bicycle, should they prove successful. My parents gave me only one piece of advice, "Do your best, we don't expect any more of you."

Whether or not I did do my best remains to be seen but suffice to say that I passed the first examination but failed the second. The next year I was allowed to re-sit the grammar school test as a 12 year old. This time I passed the first examination and was borderline for the second examination. This meant I was granted an interview which, together with the school's report on my ability, would decide my fate. I felt the interview went well. I had some impressive class exercise books to show the panel, many containing high marks for arithmetic and English done in the classroom. However, I did not pass the interview. Many years later I heard from other pupils who had suffered the same experience at Holy Rood School, that the school always gave favourable reports to children of families whom they considered to be "good Catholics". My father's reluctance to send his children to a Catholic school and his threat to have the two eldest children confirmed in the Protestant faith, obviously had repercussions for me!

The decision to send me to the Catholic school now seemed to have been a disaster. Almost all my friends from Even Swindon school passed the examination and went to grammar school. I was fated to remain at the elementary school, judged insufficiently academic to study at a higher level and thereby destined for an unskilled or semi-skilled career.

I was determined to prove everyone wrong. Fortunately my parents felt the same and recognised that I had the same ability as my sisters. In their opinion I ought to be able to cope with a grammar school education. Although money was quite "tight", my father agreed to send me to Our Lady's Convent School, a small fee-paying Catholic girls' grammar school in Cirencester. Although this would entail a 15-mile journey each day, my father would be able to get cheap travel for me on the railway so the travelling would not be an undue problem. However, being another Catholic school, the time-table was scheduled so that the first lesson each day was religious instruction, and as my train would mean my arriving between 10 and 20 minutes late each day, the school would not accept me because I would miss such "vital instruction".

Not wishing to give up on the idea of getting me to a grammar school, my father then wrote to his old grammar school in Cirencester. The school seemed keen to consider the daughter of an ex-pupil and, not having filled all the available places from local grammar school test successes, agreed for me to visit the school and take an examination, which would be followed by an interview with the Headmaster.

I was not nervous at this prospect. I had always seen examinations as a challenge and certainly nothing to fear; rather a chance to prove my worth. I clearly remember writing a composition in the examination and not knowing whether to use "el" or "le" for the ending of the word "cattle".

One of the first questions asked of me in the interview was, "How do you spell 'cattle'?"

Guessing that what I had chosen to write — "el" — was incorrect, I replied, "c-a-t-t-l-e."

"Why did you write 'c-a-t-t-e-l'?" was the Headmaster's query.

"I guess I was careless, or nervous," I replied. "Of course I know how to spell 'cattle'."

The rest of the interview went well and my father was called in and told that a place was available for me to start in September. The explanation that, having to travel from Swindon by train each day, would mean I would be up to 20 minutes late for school proved no problem and the Headmaster wished me luck in my future studies.

At the end of August my parents were getting concerned that they had not been informed of the starting date or of the school uniform they were to purchase. My father wrote to the school, explained the result of my examination and interview and the verbal promise of a place for September. To our dismay a reply was received to the effect that the Headmaster had tragically died during the summer holidays and there was no record of his promise of a place.

Sadly, I was destined to remain at Holy Rood for the next two years and would receive only a rudimentary education. Thus it was that I continued with the uninspiring, non-academic educational programme. However, I must have shown academic flare since, without increased effort, I was awarded third prize in

Standard 5 and had attained top of the class before I left the school.

There were some new subjects added to the curriculum for the last two years of elementary education. For one day each week the girls studied domestic science and the boys woodwork. With no facilities in the school for teaching these subjects we attended special centres. The girls did domestic science at Lincoln Street Centre. This was a two-storey building which largely resembled a normal house but which had two large rooms containing sinks, large wooden tables and cookers, together with other kitchen equipment. We wore a cap and apron and studied housewifery prior to being let loose on cookery lessons.

The teacher at Lincoln Street was a Miss Clark, a real ogre. We were all terrified of her.

"You, Margaret, will clean the brass stair rods."

Thank goodness. I'd been given a relatively easy task. No chance to get this wrong and incur the wrath of Miss Clark. I duly collected all the rods from the stairs leading to the first floor and brought them back to the "kitchen". Armed with two clean dusters and a tin of Brasso, I was working industriously when a voice behind me bellowed, "One at a time, girl."

I was too terrified to enquire what was meant by this order. Nobody in their right mind tried to polish two rods at once. I was doing them "one at a time". I continued to apply Brasso to one rod, polish it and then tackle the next one. Surely that was correct.

A few minutes later the voice bellowed at me again.

"I said one at a time. What if someone comes down the stairs while you have all the rods in here?"

It dawned on me — the rods kept the stair carpet in place. What I was supposed to do was take up one rod, bring it to the kitchen, clean it, return it to its place and bring the next. Fortunately the task took me most of the morning and I guess the physical exercise involved did me a power of good.

When we started cookery lessons things got even worse. I had no aptitude or expertise in the subject, largely due to my lack of patience. Custard and gravy was always lumpy, jelly never set and stew resembled an insipid, greasy slime.

One day, one of the girls was not paying attention to Miss Clark. To attract her attention, and by way of reprimand, Miss Clark picked up a saucepan lid and threw it at her. The girl ducked and the saucepan lid went straight through the window. Miss Clark merely carried on the lesson as though nothing had happened, apart from sending one girl, with dustpan and brush, to clear up the broken glass. We were too startled to see the funny side at the time but the relating of the story later always resulted in hoots of laughter.

I hated domestic science and got out of the lessons as often as possible. At one point I cut my finger on some glass at home. I can assure you, as far as Miss Clark was informed, that cut was very bad and the finger stayed bandaged well beyond its healed state, thus ensuring my being excused from lessons at Lincoln Street.

Suffice it to say that the last two years at Holy Rood school passed relatively painlessly — apart from one incident.

Although in Mr. Corrigan's class (the most senior of the school), we were ordered, one afternoon, to report to Sister Concepta's class after break. We were not told why but assumed Mr. Corrigan was unavailable to teach us. Not wanting to be demoted by being combined with Standard 5 pupils, we pretended not to remember the instruction and, ten minutes into the lesson were still to be found, unsupervised in our own classroom.

I will not suggest that I was a well-behaved pupil at all times but I had suggested that we ought to do as we were told and had persuaded a few others to move, with me, next door. Just at this moment, Sister Concepta appeared at the door wielding a cane above her head. She was clearly in an uncontrollable rage at being so blatantly defied. She let rip with the cane at the nearest pupils and caught me across the back of my bare legs. I was in considerable pain but felt it useless to try to reason with a woman in such a temper.

When I arrived home my mother was furious. The weal was now a one-inch long raised piece of flesh turning various shades of red and blue. Although usually a very quiet, restrained woman, my mother would always rise to the defence of her children. Next morning she marched me back to school and showed Sister Concepta the weal. Sister Concepta apologised saying she had merely lost her temper.

"Does our religion teach us we can lose our temper?" my mother enquired.

"No," was the reply, followed by more apologies.

"You dare strike my daughter again for any reason and I'll report you to the Director of Education." With that Mum turned on her heels and flounced from the room.

On reflection, I guess Holy Rood School was glad to see the back of me and secretly pleased they had only encountered one of the Wood girls.

Canon Noonan did give me a reference when I left school. It simply said:

"Margaret has attended this school and is a good girl."

I never felt this helped me to secure any jobs!

CHAPTER
EIGHT

The Effects of the War

Countless books have been written recalling the horror, and sometimes humour, of the Second World War and how it affected the lives of British people. I want to relate how I remember this era and how it affected my own family. It could be argued that this was a period covering some of the most formative and crucial years of my life. In 1939 I was nine years old. By the time the war ended in 1946, I was 15 years old and should have chosen, and embarked on, my life-long career.

The date was 3rd September 1939 — a quiet, peaceful, late-summer Sunday morning. I was in Mum's bedroom helping her make the bed. Dad was downstairs listening to the radio. At 11 o'clock the Prime Minister, Mr. Neville Chamberlain, made his famous broadcast to the nation ending with the words ". . . we are now at war with Germany."

Mum sighed. I looked out of the window. Nothing had changed. The street was as quiet as most Sundays. People did not come rushing out of their houses at this news. I had no idea what "being at war" meant; as a 9 year-old who had recently started at a new school, I had more important things on my mind.

Things became clearer the next weekend when Auntie Win and Uncle Laurie came, from London, for a weekend visit. Auntie Win was in tears.

"We had an air raid warning last night," she said. "It turned out to be a false alarm but we were all scared. I'm worried for my boys. George and Jim are bound to be called up for the armed forces. It's all right for you and Geoff, you have all girls. I could lose both my oldest boys."

I could see that Mum found it difficult to commiserate with her sister, not being in the same situation. As it transpired, war was to have a devastating effect on us all but fortunately George and Jim survived the conflict, despite serving in the RAF and "seeing action" on numerous occasions.

The first intrusion into our lives was the issue of gas masks. Fearing the use of poisonous gas by the Germans, it had been decided to issue every British citizen with a gas mask and provide instructions on how to use it.

Local ARP (air raid precaution) wardens were quickly recruited and trained in each neighbourhood. I remember Mr Stafford, our next door neighbour, was one of the first to volunteer. These wardens had many duties among which was to see that the blackout was observed, that houses were made as safe as possible — strips of paper being placed across windows to prevent glass splintering if broken — and to distribute and fit gas masks. Later they issued houses with stirrup pumps and sand bags where appropriate.

The gas masks were quite hideous and rather frightening to wear at first, but we all had so many practices that I am sure, had there been a gas attack, we could have donned them quickly and survived in them for a considerable amount of time. Children up to about 5 years of age had gas masks fashioned to look like Mickey Mouse. For babies, a cot mask was provided into which the mother was expected to place the baby and then pump air continuously into the contraption. One wonders how many mothers would have been calm enough to keep the flow of air constant, had an attack actually happened.

We were instructed to carry our gas masks at all times. They were provided in a stout cardboard box with string attached. It was obvious that this box would soon deteriorate so most people made covers for the box with a shoulder strap. ARP wardens and other hastily recruited personnel had more sophisticated gas masks which were packed in canvas-webbing bags. Gas masks soon became part of our attire and we donned them whenever we left the house. To arrive at school without one's gas mask was a punishable offence.

The blackout was a deterrent to German night raids. It was felt that if everything was in darkness, German planes would be unable to locate towns or other areas worth bombing. All street lights were banned. Shop windows could not be lit. Houses had to have thick black curtains to pull across all windows when the lights were on in the house. Even when opening the outside door of the house a curtain had to be pulled or the light switched off so that no chink of light emerged.

All vehicles, including bicycles, could display only dimmed lights, pointed to shine in just one spot. You can imagine the number of minor accidents which occurred until people became used to the blackout.

The curbs of pavements were painted white so that people could locate them in the dark. Most people carried a torch when out walking but even these had to be properly dimmed. In some areas the farmers painted white stripes on their cows so that they could locate them for early morning milking in the winter.

Mum spent hours making dark curtains for all our windows. Old sheets and blankets were dyed and we all lent a hand in putting them up. Eventually, my ever-inventive Dad made black shutters out of stiff black card framed by plywood. These were fitted tight to the windows and held in place with wooden clips.

Identity cards were introduced at this time. Everyone had a number. The same basic number was used for each household, the last number being the one which identified the owner's position in the family. Identity cards had to be carried at all times.

AIR RAIDS

Swindon's first experience of an air raid warning came during the night of 25th June 1940, Win's birthday and the day on which she took her first Matriculation examination. Our sleep was somewhat disturbed since we all got up, went downstairs and wondered what we should do next. Fortunately nothing happened. However, we were to experience many other sleepless nights because, quite often, the sirens would sound when the German planes flew over Swindon en route to other city targets, such as Coventry. Later in the night another alert would be sounded as the planes flew overhead on their return journey. It is thought that some of the bombs dropped on Swindon may have been stray bombs jettisoned by these German planes returning from other raids.

The air raid warning was quite "scary". At the first alert to a raid, the siren would wail in a droning rising and falling wave of sound. For this purpose the GWR steam hooter was used. This could be heard within about a 20-mile radius, so living only about a mile from it, we had no chance of sleeping through an alert. At the beginning of the alert, ARP wardens patrolled each street blowing intermittent blasts on their whistles. The end of the raid was signalled by the same hooter and whistles but this time by a long continuous blast.

Fortunately, Swindon never suffered the devastating bombing which some of the cities close at hand (London, Bath, Bristol) endured. However, Swindon was an important railway junction. The vast GWR works stopped making railway engines and other stock and turned to assembling bomber planes, making tanks and munitions. Many other factories were located in Swindon, such as the Plessey Company, or close by, such as Vickers-Armstrong at South Marston. Added to this, the air bases of Fairford and Lyneham were only a few miles away. There was always the chance that the

Germans would seek to bomb this considerably important town.

One such factory which relocated to Swindon at this time was Short Brothers — a firm which also made war weapons. This factory had been bombed out of its previous locations and so came to the relatively "safe" town of Swindon. Ironically, almost as soon as it was established, Swindon became the target for German bombers. There was much speculation that spies had infiltrated the firm and were sending valuable information to the Germans.

Short Brothers' factory was relatively close to Bruce Street, where we lived. Added to this, one of the main railway lines ran along the end of our street. With the GWR already in the area, it is no wonder that a lot of the bombing of Swindon was around our area. In total some 48 lives were lost and more than 100 people were injured in the Swindon bombing. Some 50 homes were destroyed.

Some amusing events resulted from these air raids. On one occasion there had been an early morning raid in which the gasometer, at the other side of the railway line from Bruce Street, had been set on fire. Gas escaped from this huge storage tank and filled the air. Mrs. Stafford called over the garden fence, "Mrs Wood, could you let me have a shilling for my gas meter? I haven't enough gas left to boil a kettle for breakfast."

We all fell about laughing and suggested she brought her kettle out into the garden and lit the air with a match.

All single adults were expected to do some kind of "war duties" in addition to their day jobs. Kath was enrolled as a Fire Watcher. This was a lesser form of ARP warden. One of her jobs was to patrol the street on the sounding of an air raid alert and make sure everyone had heard the warning and were going to shelters, where necessary.

One day the air raid alert sounded and we prepared to go to our shelter.

"Where's Kath?" Mum enquired.

"Don't know," we all chorused.

"Well, look for her. She should be out on duty."

Kath was eventually found. She was sitting under the Morrison shelter (a large iron table shelter which we had in the living room) resplendent in her tin hat! So much for Kath's bravery in the face of an enemy attack!

One early morning raid was on Ferndale Road, not far from Bruce Street where we lived. It happened just after Dad had left for "duty" at the works — he was a trained ambulance man and had to report to his works' station as soon as the air raid siren sounded. One of his colleagues had had to travel from Moredon, some three miles away and so was late getting to the works, well after the bombs had landed on Ferndale Road. He recounted how much of Ferndale Road was on fire.

"What about Bruce Street?" Dad enquired frantically.

"Don't know about that," was the reply, "I didn't look down there."

Seeing Dad's distress, his superior allowed him to return home to make sure we were all safe.

Although we had been frightened by the noise and tremors caused by the bombs falling so close, we were all quite safe in the Anderson shelter Dad had erected for us in the back garden. However, we never forgot Dad's face as he ran down the garden path. He was as white as a sheet and could barely speak. This minor incident served to give us an insight into what traumas people in the heavily bombed areas were undergoing.

Not only did the government attempt to provide all homes with some form of shelter, but they also erected large shelters in public places. Faringdon Road Park was one such area. There, the council built three enormous concrete shelters. They were dark and damp inside but, hopefully, would protect people from the blast of nearby bombs.

Having to make a two-mile journey to school each day, Mum must have been worried about my safety at such times. Quite often the air raid warning did sound whilst I was en route. One day it sounded as I was walking home after school. It happened to be a long raid and I didn't arrive home until well after tea-time.

"Where on earth have you been?" Mum enquired. "I've been worried out of my mind."

"In the shelter in the Park," I told her.

I wondered what all the fuss was about. Hadn't I done what I was supposed to do? Why did she need to worry? I guess I never found the answer to this until I had my own children and learned to worry over far less trivial incidents in which they were involved.

Naturally air raids often took place whilst we were at school. Every school had a well-rehearsed drill in place for such eventualities. As far as Holy Rood School was concerned, at the sound of the air raid warning we all left school and lined up in the boys' playground before being dispersed to neighbouring houses where we took shelter.

We older pupils were designated Team Leaders and were responsible for gathering together the five or six children assigned to us from the younger classes before marching them across to our designated "shelter". One day we were engaged in this process of lining up when a German plane flew overhead, closely pursued by one of our Spitfires. The latter was firing at the German but, sadly, all the bullets were falling over the top of the enemy plane and landing in front of it. Several went through the windows of our neighbouring school, The College. It was then that the teachers, realizing the potential danger, shouted, "Get back into the school — unless you are ready to go to your houses."

A chaotic scene evolved. Pupils were crashing into each other as some tried to go one way, into the school, others, dragging five or six little ones behind them, tried to get out of the one inadequate gate. With my "charges" I reached my "safe house" in a matter of seconds and banged on the door.

"All right, I'm coming. What's the hurry?"

The door was opened by the lady of the house who was quite oblivious to the minor battle taking place in the skies above us.

The last bombs to fall on Swindon were in Drove Road on 29th August 1942.

94

HOLY ROOD'S NUMBERS RISE

Early on in the war children were evacuated from major cities for fear of the devastating loss of life which would result from German air raids. A number of these children came to Swindon. The Catholics among them had to attend Holy Rood School and the pupil numbers increased alarmingly. Classrooms were over-crowded. Sometimes there were three to a desk.

One day we had the customary head inspection by a visiting nurse, nicknamed "Nitty Nora" who inspected each pupil for head lice. The parents of a pupil found to have such insects was sent a letter and told to keep the child from school until the hair was rid of the infection. I arrived home one day to find Mum in a right state.

"What's this?" she enquired of me, brandishing a letter.

"I don't know," I said. "It looks like a letter. Who is it from?"

"The school," was the reply. "It says you've got 'nits'."

"Oh!" was all I could think of saying. I recalled "Nitty Nora's" visit but couldn't explain why I had been singled out. Was it something I had done?

I think it was Mum's first encounter with what was looked upon as a "dirty head". I was marched off to the doctor who explained to Mum that nits were the eggs of head lice and that these could hop from one head to another very easily and preferred to lay their eggs in clean hair. He explained to Mum how to wash my hair in Derback soap and use a scurf comb to extract the

95

eggs which he showed her were sticking to the strands of hair. He also advised treating the whole family as a precaution. Within a few days my hair was rid of the "beasts" and I returned to school accompanied by Mum who had a good few words to say about them infecting her daughter!

Sister Concepta explained, "Unfortunately we have a lot of evacuees in the school. Many of them come from the East End of London. Margaret sits next to one such girl. That's who she will have got it from."

To poor Sister Concepta's surprise, this did little to placate Mum who, instead of accepting the explanation, rose to the defence of the evacuees accusing Sister Concepta.

"How dare you tar all evacuees with the same brush, or suggest that just because they come from a poor part of London they are dirty."

I sometimes think Sister Concepta felt she couldn't win with my mother.

RATIONING

It was always obvious that, being a country which imported most of its food supplies, there would be difficulties in trying to feed the population now that the merchant shipping was under attack by German U-boats and other enemy ships.

Advertisements sprang up urging people to "Dig For Victory". Most people heeded this message. The aim was, of course, for each family to be as self-sufficient as possible. Dad already had a very productive allotment but now he dug up our small but very useful back lawn and planted potatoes.

Pupils in Standard 7 of Holy Rood School had a new lesson added to their time-table — gardening. Some allotments were rented and Mr Corrigan took charge. By the time I arrived in Standard 7, the project was successfully underway. I loved our gardening afternoons, despite the fact that we had quite a long walk there and back carrying a selection of gardening tools. Dad had instilled a love of growing vegetables in the whole family through his enthusiasm for his own allotment.

The project taught pupils a number of skills. We learned how to dig, plant the seeds, propagate plants, sow, hoe, weed and gather in the produce. This was sold within the school so the pupils were responsible for fixing prices, keeping accounts and using the proceeds to buy more seeds.

Despite the best endeavours at self-sufficiency, it was evident that rationing of certain foods was inevitable. Very early in the war things such as sugar, tea, dairy produce and meat were rationed. Each person had a ration book which had to be taken when shopping for food. A coupon was cut from the book, or a cross made in it, every time a purchase of the weekly allocation was made so it was very difficult to get extra amounts. The rations were very meagre, for example each person was allowed 2 oz each of cheese, butter, and fat, 8 oz of sugar and 2 oz of tea. Each person was allocated 1 fresh egg per fortnight and 1 lb of jam every 2 months. The government was quick to produce recipe books showing how to use powdered eggs and dried milk, which were not rationed, and to make fat-free cakes.

People, surprisingly, adjusted quite quickly to these restraints and made light of their problems. Mrs Patten was a neighbour who often called on Mum for a chat. On leaving one afternoon she announced, "I'm off home to have a bit of 'Oh-be-joyful' for my tea."

We all laughed but knew what she meant. She was going to have bread and butter — a real luxury. It was so much of a luxury that few people ate bread with butter and jam on it. Mum always said, "You can have butter or jam. Which will it be?"

If we had a sandwich there was never any butter on the bread. That would have been far too wasteful.

"What are you going to give up for Lent?" Mum enquired of us girls.

"Don't know," we replied. We had given up so much food already we didn't see why we should have to do further penance of this kind during Lent.

"What about giving up sugar in your tea?" Mum suggested. "I could give the sugar we save to Auntie Marty. She needs far more sugar than her ration. In return she will give me some of the eggs and dripping she gets from the farmers who come into her shop."

The result: we got to eat the occasional boiled egg, Mum could do a roast dinner occasionally and we never took sugar in tea again.

Food not deemed a necessity was not rationed but was in very short supply. Sweets (later rationed), jelly, sausages, oranges etc would sometimes appear in a shop and were quickly snapped up. People formed queues at such shops and would wait, sometimes as long as an hour, to reach the counter only to be told, "Sorry, that was the last."

Whenever one saw a queue one tended to join it — often not knowing for some time what you were queuing for! If I was in town with Mum and we saw a queue she would join it and say, "Get behind me. Here's some money. Whatever it is, get it. I'll meet you over there afterwards."

Thus is was that we managed to get double our share. If it was evident that two people from the same family were being served it could have started a riot, hence Mum and I were "strangers" until we met again later.

Bananas were not available at all during the war. The importation of this non-essential food was considered a waste of valuable shipping space. Hence many children did not see a banana until they were five or six years old. After the war stories were told of young children trying to eat this strange fruit with the skin still intact. Many decades later, I used to tell my own children about our lack of bananas during the war until the sight of a banana on the table would give rise to a chorus from them to the effect: "Wait for it . . . 'during the war I never tasted a banana'."

Later in the war more and more things were added to those which were "rationed". Bread, cigarettes, clothes were just a few of the other things which succumbed to rationing.

JOBS

Win eventually gained her School Certificate from grammar school and went to Teacher Training College in Bristol from 1941–43. It cost Dad £50 per annum in fees, not to mention the fact that Win's availability to gain paid employment was deferred until she was 20 years of age. This was a great financial burden for Dad but he managed to pay the fees because of the extra overtime he earned when the GWR was engaged in war work.

I remember visiting Win whilst she was at College in Bristol. Both Bath and Bristol endured many heavy raids. Win can recall the fires over Bath and Bristol lighting up the sky for miles around. On one such occasion we traversed the railway line above one of Bath's streets in great trepidation. There had been a heavy raid the night before and the area of the railway station had been particularly targeted. The train inched its way precariously along the line spanning the main road and into the shattered station.

As a qualified teacher, Win was considered to be in a "reserved occupation", so was not forced to join one of the armed forces, the Land Army, or work in a factory as was the case for most women of her age conscripted to aid the war effort. She was, however, forced to do one night of Fire Watching duty each week. This meant she had to report to one of the neighbourhood schools and sleep there for the night in case of a raid and bombing in the area. In such cases schools were often used as reception centres for the homeless.

Kath was working as a secretary in a firm of chartered accountants called Burgess, Burgess & Co. This was not a reserved occupation so she, and her boss, were directed to office work at the Vickers-Armstrong factory at South Marston. Auntie Poppie eventually joined her there since, as a Lady's Maid, she was not in a reserved occupation and was forced into some form of war work. She lived with us for the period of her employment at Vickers-Armstrong. Auntie Freda escaped conscription into war work by choosing to stay at home to look after her ailing mother, Granny Wood.

LEISURE PURSUITS

Few people took holidays throughout the war years. It was sufficient to be able to visit close relatives occasionally to exchange war experiences or check on each other's safety.

It wasn't possible to have the usual summer holidays by the sea because most coastal towns were "out of bounds" in case of German invasion. Anyway, the beaches were covered in barbed wire and had guns positioned on them. Some of the beaches on the south east coast even got shelled by Germans occupying the channel ports of France.

We continued our normal family pursuits of listening to records and the wireless. To aid our interpretation of the news bulletins, we had a large map of Europe displayed on the dining room wall. Dad would avidly plot the progress of troops, our own and the enemy's, on this map.

101

We girls were all good knitters so we helped Mum to knit for the armed forces. The government provided wool and patterns and we undertook the making of such things as socks, gloves and Balaclava helmets.

We continued to go on cycle rides, although long, unfamiliar routes were avoided since all the road signs had been removed as a deterrent to the progress of any possible German invasion.

Looking back on the war years, one appreciates what an austere time this was and how lucky we were to have been spared the traumas of evacuation or the intense bombing which devastated such places as London. Indeed the war years bred a generation of thrifty people who would go out of their way to help a neighbour in distress. It also further developed the sense of humour and "stiff upper lip" attitude to life's problems which was already a part of the British culture.

CHAPTER
NINE

Continuing Education

"If my name had been Wee Georgie Wood (*a famous comedian often heard on the wireless at this time*) instead of Geoffrey George Wood, I might have considered it. As it is you will just have to learn some bread and butter skills and earn a decent living."

"But, Dad . . . it's all I've ever wanted to do."

As my fourteenth birthday and the school leaving date approached, my parents began to pester me about a career. I couldn't see what all the fuss was about. I had made up my mind I was going to be an actress. For this I needed to audition for a place at drama school and approached my parents with this request.

My father laughed, but secretly he was sorry that he could not help me to fulfil my dreams. I learned later that he had in fact made enquiries about the cost of a course at a drama school, but the fees were quite out of the question. Hence it was that, reluctantly, I agreed to forget my dreams . . . at least for the moment. I was not one to give up easily.

Thus it was that I found myself, once again, armed with pen, pencil and ruler embarking on another day of

103

examinations, this time for entry to Day Commercial Classes at The College.

I remember that day quite clearly. To start with, the course for which I was seeking entrance and, of course, the entrance examination was held in the same building as one of the three Swindon grammar schools. At last I was to have the chance to be educated in a building which oozed academic excellence. It was an impressive four-storey building with proper science rooms (not that my course of study would include any science subjects) and a well-equipped gymnasium. The classrooms were furnished with individual desks. What heaven! A real "college", not just a school.

The examination consisted of three subjects, English, Arithmetic and General Knowledge. The English paper was a joy. We were asked, among other things, to write a composition entitled "My Future Career". I wrote enthusiastically about the theatre and my career as an actress. I wrote of the sheer delight of being able to study and portray such diverse characters, to be someone different with each play I performed; the joy of entertaining; the rapturous applause with which my every performance would be greeted; the fame; the fortune; the name in lights. It didn't occur to me that the Principal of the Course might have sought candidates who were keen to train for a career in office work!

My parents were delighted when the results were announced and I was offered a place on the two-year course commencing the following September. I sometimes wonder why they never worried about my persistently stressing that I was taking the course to please them but had no intention of working in an office.

The next eighteen months were spent, not unhappily, learning shorthand, typewriting, accounts and various other office-related subjects.

I had always envied my sister Win who, attending The College Grammar School, had been expected to wear a uniform, albeit a hideous black gym-slip with white blouse and long, black stockings but with a school hat with badge and band.

My dream was soon shattered when I took my first step into that hallowed building. Day Commercial Classes were housed in the same building as the grammar school, but did not use the same rooms. Instead of the longed-for individual desks, we used rooms on the top floor of this four-storey building which were furnished with very long wooden tables stretching the complete width of the room, at which students sat on uncomfortably high wooden stools. The only individual desks were in the typing room.

Since space was limited, we were sometimes forced to use the odd science laboratory not immediately needed by the grammar school. Many a time a page of my shorthand notebook got soaked as it was flipped over into a sink which housed a dripping tap.

Best of all was physical education. We were allowed to use the gymnasium belonging to the grammar school. Until now, I had not seen a fully-equipped gymnasium. Wall-bars, ropes, boxes, vaulting horses were all new to me but I lapped up the chance to master them, unlike many of my friends who, now they were over fourteen years of age, considered themselves too lady-like to enjoy such physical activities.

Another dream came true — at last I got to carry a satchel. We used lots of different books for the new subjects and were issued with our own copies and expected to take them to lessons and use them for homework (another phenomenon which was new to me).

I had waited years to emulate my sister and my grammar school friends and, although a little disappointed at the environment, determined to enjoy the next two years.

The classes were quite small, about half the size of the classes at Holy Rood. They were mixed but, by nature of the career prospects, most of the students were girls. It was interesting to meet people from different schools and different backgrounds and to be treated almost as adults. At least we were on the course voluntarily so staff tried to inspire us rather than merely keep us gainfully occupied.

I got on well with most of the teachers. It was a joy to have to move from room to room for different lessons and to have a proper time-table to adhere to with a different teacher for almost every different subject.

Art was never a favourite subject of mine. For one thing I was hopeless at drawing and only adequate at painting, writing in script, and other forms of art to which we had been introduced in Standard 7 at Holy Rood School.

"For homework, I want you to design a cover for the school magazine." This was how the art teacher ensured that we all got involved with the project.

"The Principal has agreed to award a prize for the person whose design is eventually chosen," she continued.

I had been in Assembly when the Principal announced that there was to be a school magazine and was determined to write something for publication. The cover would be left to those with an artistic leaning. I was not interested. However, there was still the question of my art homework to be completed.

"Win, could you do my art homework for me?" I pleaded.

"What is it?" she enquired.

"To design a cover for the school magazine."

"I don't know what to draw," Win complained in the vain hope that she would not be persuaded to perform this illicit task.

"Oh, just put a typewriter, a pen and inkwell and ruler and some accounts books at the bottom and the name Day Commercial Classes in a semi-circle around the top," I suggested.

Win was never one to refuse to do a favour and was infinitely better at drawing than I was. So, the next day I handed in my art homework and forgot about the incident. About two weeks later the Principal announced during morning assembly, before the whole school:

"We have the winner of the design for the magazine cover."

As usual, I was paying very little attention. Then I heard:

"The runner up is Veronica Hanson. Her fine, indeed, intricate design, showed real talent."

There was enthusiastic applause as Veronica made her way to the platform to receive her runner-up prize and her design was duly displayed to an enthusiastic and appreciative audience.

"And now for the winning design . . ." the Principal continued, "A design which is simple, yet so appropriate for this publication. I am pleased to announce that our winner is . . . Margaret Wood."

Still in a daze as my friends prodded and pushed me out of my seat, I found myself advancing towards the platform where I was greeted by a bold handshake from the Principal and given my prize — a box containing watercolour paints and brushes.

I feared my bright red face would betray my embarrassment. But, ever the polished actress, I accepted my prize graciously and returned to my seat with head held high to the applause of the whole school and spirited congratulations from my closer friends (most of whom, I am sure, guessed this had not been my own work.)

I couldn't wait to get home and tell Win of my success. She was not really pleased — just insisted that I hand over the prize to her. I felt this was a bit unfair but agreed, knowing that I would have no use for a set of paints and brushes.

I was almost "caught out" when, next lesson, the art teacher told me I would have to repeat this design, this time on to a waxed stencil so that it could be reproduced on the ink duplicator. Quick-thinking as ever, I suggested I take it home and do it for homework rather than waste valuable class time on the task. Win was not pleased with the second request but, being Win, did my homework just once more.

I guess my favourite lesson remained English. We had an excellent teacher, Miss Hallard. Although most of the lessons were of formal grammar and business correspondence we did some literature and, at the end of the first year, produced a school play to which the general public were invited. I was given the lead role — that of St. Michael. It was only a one-act play but I was delighted to be picked from the whole school to play the lead.

Miss Hallard always set vocabulary for Tuesday's English homework. We were given ten words for which we had to write out the dictionary definition, learn the spelling and make up sentences to show the meaning of each word. The trouble was that Mum, persuaded by me, of course, had booked two permanent tickets for the Swindon Playhouse Repertory Company each Tuesday. Attendance at these performances proved the highlight of my week and the inspiration for my continued aspiration to become a famous actress. Hence, I spent the interval, during the performance doing my English homework. So diligent was I for fear my mother would cancel my theatre trip that I invariably got maximum marks for this particular homework.

I was so envious of the actors and actresses who made up the Swindon Repertory Company that I often came home from the Tuesday production in floods of tears — tears of sheer frustration and envy.

"If I am going to have this every time you go to a play, I will stop you going," was Mum's threat.

Nobody, not even my parents, could appreciate how desperate I was to emulate those professional actors and actresses.

Another teacher who inspired us all was Mr. McKinley, a young, attractive, Scot who taught us Commerce and Accounts. He regaled us with humorous tales of when he was a shop assistant in a big London department store. He also taught us how to forge signatures, though not sufficiently expertly to ensure we could embark upon a life-time of crime.

I took to Shorthand reasonably well although hated the long hours of practice and learning of short forms set for homework by an uninspiring teacher. Indeed I always vowed that I hated Shorthand so much that I would never teach it. Little did I know that that was to be one of the main subjects I would eventually teach.

Half-way through the course our shorthand teacher was replaced by a man, a Mr. Wright, who came to us from Brighton Technical College. He was an excellent teacher of shorthand but had very strong principles. For one thing, he insisted we should write our shorthand notes in ink. We had been taught from the outset to use a pencil pointed at both ends, in case of mishap during dictation. Most of us had become used to a pencil and were not prepared to ask our parents to

110

buy us the special fountain pen he recommended. A few of us, including me, decided to "go on strike". If he would not let us use a pencil, we did not write. Eventually we won the day. He relented and some of us went on to achieve high speeds — still using a pencil.

Our first typewriting lesson was a frightening experience. We lined up outside a room which had some twenty or thirty wooden desks.

"Now, how many of you will be getting a job with the Great Western Railway when you leave here?"

Miss Foster, a white-haired, straight-backed lady with pince nez glasses perched on the end of her nose, put this question to a trembling line of first term students.

A few hands shot up.

"Come with me," she barked.

These privileged students filed in and took their allocated seats.

"The rest of you, go in quietly and take up the remaining desks."

We meekly did as we were told, wondering where the typewriters were.

"All stand. Push back your chairs. Take hold of the handle at the front of the desk. Pull it gently upwards."

So Miss Foster instructed us how to gain access to the typewriter which we could now see was housed in a covered well-desk.

"Now take hold of the pieces of protruding wood at each side of the flap on which the typewriter is housed. Pull them gently upwards and towards you. Now, push

111

the whole platform, containing the typewriter, back until it locks in position."

Low and behold, the typewriter appeared housed on a flat surface which, when correctly rotated and pushed backwards, provided a very firm base.

"Now we will reverse the process to put the machine away."

I doubt whether much more was accomplished in that first lesson but we were all confidently able to access and re-house our machines each lesson with the minimum of noise and no fuss or mishaps.

Needless to say, none of us had a choice of typewriter. We merely accepted whatever machine was housed in the closed desk we had chosen when we first entered the room except, of course, those "important" students who knew that they had sufficient "contacts" to get them a career in the offices of the Great Western Railway. Now the reason for their preferential treatment became obvious. The GWR was the only employer in the town to still be equipped with Oliver three-bank typewriters. These machines had three banks of keys and a double shift system, shift keys having to be used for capital letters and for figures. The more modern typewriters had four banks of keys, the fourth bank housing the figures and extra characters thus using only a single shift system. The home keys, which every touch typist used as the basis for locating all the other keys, included the semi-colon key, struck with the little finger on the right hand. The Oliver three-bank machines did not have the semi-colon in that position, hence operators of this machine learned a different set of home keys. All the Oliver machines were located on one side of the room and these were the desks now occupied by the prospective GWR employees.

Fate must have been smiling on me for that first lesson. I was lucky to be allocated an LC Smith machine with a left-hand carriage return — one of the most popular machines. I got to love my typing lessons and progressed effortlessly.

As we became more proficient, we were introduced to Speed and Accuracy Tests. These involved typing as fast as possible for ten minutes without stopping to make corrections. At the end of the ten minutes, we were shown how to calculate our speed, mark errors and find the resulting net speed, which was often the benchmark used at interviews for jobs and for entry to external examinations.

It must be remembered that, at this time, the war was still on and Swindon was still subject to air raids.

"We are now going to do a ten minute speed and accuracy test," Miss Foster announced.

"Insert a clean sheet, turn to page 1 and prepare to concentrate. I shall say 'Go' to commence. You will then type accurately as fast as you can. You will not stop for any reason. If the air raid siren sounds, keep on typing. If the bombs start falling, keep on typing. If the roof is blown off, I may allow you to stop and take shelter but you will await my command."

Miss Foster ("Fossy" to her students) was such a stern individual that we were reluctant to assume she was joking.

"Sit up straight, eyes on the copy. Go."

The clatter of a roomful of typewriters would probably have drowned the sound of any air raid alert but we all heard Miss Foster call, "Stop."

Instantly silence reigned. Paper was pulled noiselessly from the machine and the process of calculating net speed was explained and carried out.

Most future lessons began with keyboard drills conducted with fingers housed under huge black metal shields to ensure no peeping at the keys. Next followed the nerve-racking speed and accuracy test.

Not being of a nervous disposition, I enjoyed even this part of the lessons and progressed quickly in the subject. I even got on friendly terms with "Fossy" — all due to Kath's influence. After leaving school at fourteen, Kath had enrolled at evening classes and learnt to type under the direction of Miss Foster. She had warned me of this teacher's severity but assured me that she was an excellent teacher from whom I would learn much. To help me gain the teacher's attention and put me into her "good books", Kath sent a little present via me to her old teacher.

"Give her this pound of sugar and say it's from an old student," Kath suggested.

In view of the rationing, a pound of sugar was indeed a welcomed gift.

"Which student is that?" Miss Foster enquired.

I explained that my sister had been a student of her evening class.

"Ah, Kathleen. I remember her. An excellent typist. I hope you will do as well, Margaret."

"So do I," I replied. "Kath has already passed her Intermediate and Advanced RSA examinations. I intend to do the same but want to know what I can do after that."

"Well, I guess that eventually you could take the Teacher's Diploma but for that you have to be very, very good."

"I'll do it, just you see." I promised. And I did . . . just five years later.

In the second term of the course, I was called to the Head of the Commerce Department's office. I tapped on the door and a deep voice boomed, "Come."

On entering I came face to face with Mr. Sladen, a white-haired, distinguished-looking gentleman and the much-respected Head.

"Well, Margaret . . ." he drawled. The elongated drawl of the word "W-e-l-l" struck fear into the heart of the most confident student.

"It seems congratulations are in order. You have passed your first RSA typewriting examination."

Handing me the "Pass" slip, he shook me so positively by the hand that my typing speed was lowered for some days to come. This was possibly my first indication that I was progressing well with my course. Just three students had been selected from the new students to sit for the first of many external examinations. We all three passed, two of us with a credit. The next term I was one of only a few who took and passed the RSA 50 wpm shorthand examination.

Other exam successes followed and suffice to say that I left the course in December 1945 with certificates in all the subjects, including my beloved English. I also managed, in my last term, to gain top place in the internal examinations, sharing the honour with Colin Eatwell who had always managed to steal the top position from me in these term examinations.

I also aspired to the position of school prefect and delighted in my break duty, standing at the top of the stairs directing recalcitrant students to "Keep to the left."

During the first term of my second year at Day Commercial Classes, I was summoned to Mr Sladen's office together with another girl from the class below me. It was explained to us that, owing to the war, there was a shortage of teachers and the government had devised a scheme called the McNair Scheme to root out children who were "late-developers" and who had missed out on a grammar school education because they failed the grammar school test. The idea was to transfer these pupils (now aged 14 years) to a grammar school and give them an express course to enable them to "catch up" and eventually matriculate in order to gain entrance to a Teacher Training College.

The two of us had been recommended and were to attend a series of examinations and interviews at the local Education Offices. We did this and both enjoyed the experience and were confident that we had been given this late chance to gain our rightful grammar school education.

Once again my hopes were dashed when, a few weeks later, the Principal had to explain to me that although I had proved suitable for the scheme, there had been so little appropriate response that the scheme was not going to take place. Fate had, once again, denied me my rightful education but it only made me more determined to prove everyone wrong.

There was an attempt, on this course, to give us some training for adult social activities. Just before Christmas our physical education lessons were changed to ballroom dancing. With so few boys on the course, the lessons were less than meaningful but we all learned the basic ballroom dances and looked forward to the Christmas Soirée at which the girls would be encouraged to wear long dresses. I enjoyed the event, especially the new dress which Mum made for me. It felt so grown up to be going to a proper soirée in a long gown.

Housed in the College buildings was a course for boys wishing to gain apprenticeship to the building trade. As was common in those days, these boys were in a separate section of the building and used a "boys only" playground at break time.

It did not take long for several of us girls to realize that the bicycle sheds were used by both sexes and that access to them during breaks could ensure illicit liaisons with these boys. My first love was a boy from this course, Graham Hitchens. We remained firm friends for a year or so after I left the course. He was quite delicate in health and did not enter the building trade but took up an apprenticeship as an organ builder and moved away from the town. Sadly he died only a few years later.

I look back on the eighteen months at Day Commercial Classes as the happiest of my school life and the qualifications gained there as the most useful. Despite my claim that I would never work in an office, my parents were right to insist I train for a useful career. The skills learned on that course were to be the ultimate entry to some of my most rewarding work.

PART THREE

ADULTHOOD

CHAPTER
TEN

Time to Earn a Living

I was so happy at Day Commercial Classes that I believe I would never have left had I not taken the "bull by the horns" during the second year of the course. My first year had been an academic success and some of my friends began to apply for, and get, office jobs during the second year. These friends continued studying at evening classes.

Accepting that, at this moment in time at least, I was not going to be able to train as a professional actress, I started applying for positions as a junior shorthand typist. My first interview was at a local Estate Agent's offices where I was offered the job as junior shorthand-typist for the princely salary of fifteen shillings a week. The hours were 9a.m.–6p.m. Monday to Friday and 9a.m.–1p.m. on Saturday. I was delighted to announce the success of the interview to my father who responded with, "How much? You must be joking. Fifteen shillings for a 44 hour week!"

I knew that office hours were longer than the school day but my happiness at being offered a position at my first attempt clouded my judgement somewhat.

"Write and tell them that they can keep their job," was Dad's advice.

"But what shall I put in the letter? I asked.

"Just say, you won't be accepting their offer of employment as you consider the salary insufficient because you had always thought that 'the labourer is worthy of his hire'."

I did just that and returned to my studies for a few more weeks. Although there was still homework to be done, I was able to pursue my developing social life and continued with the elocution lessons I had enjoyed for several years. I entered all the local musical festivals in the verse speaking, bible recitation and sight reading classes, and enjoyed modest success.

My teacher, Violet Hood, was not keen on entering her students for examinations but I eventually developed a friendship with another of her pupils, Berlydene Hunt, who was keen to obtain LAMDA (London Academy of Music and Dramatic Art) qualifications, so we were successfully entered for Bronze, Silver and Gold medal examinations.

This period saw the inauguration of a new mixed choir in Swindon, the AEU choir. My father, a member of the Amalgamated Engineering Union, and several of his work colleagues joined the choir, as did my sister, Win. A great friend of mine at Day Commercial Classes was Nora Gill. She had a beautiful soprano voice but no training. I suggested she might like to join this new choir.

"I will, if you will," was her answer.

"Me? No way. I'm almost tone deaf!"

After discussion with Dad and Win and the choir master, it was decided that Nora would be a great asset to the choir and, if I joined also, I could provide solo dramatic renditions at the concerts.

The choir went from strength to strength and performed for a variety of audiences throughout the town. I sang soprano simply because I could stand next to Nora who drowned me with her beautiful voice. Before long both Nora and I were soloists at concerts, although my solo was obviously not of a musical nature!

By the middle of the second year of my college course (1946), I again applied for office work and was successful in obtaining a post as a junior shorthand-typist with Pope Bros., a local builders. Imagine my horror to find that the only typewriter they possessed was an Oliver Three Bank, the type which had been reserved for the potential GWR employees attending our course.

It took me no more than a week to master the new contraption but, having enrolled for evening classes, I was in a dilemma as to whether to continue my studies on the four-bank typewriter on which I had been trained or change to a three-bank machine. Fate decided for me as within my first few months in the job, the secretary left, Mr. Pope bought a four-bank typewriter, and I was offered the job as his secretary.

I enjoyed office work far more than I had expected. The money was much better than I had anticipated. I started on £1 a week as a junior and got £2 a week as soon as I was appointed secretary. The hours were much shorter than my first job application. Officially they were from 9 a.m.–5 p.m. Monday to Friday and 9 a.m.–12 noon on Saturday. However, Saturday mornings were usually cut short as Mr. Pope always cleaned the two offices himself so, as soon as he had finished his work he would say, "Get yourself home. I need you out of the way to clean the office."

Work would be stashed away in double quick time and forgotten until the following Monday.

Although I continued evening classes in shorthand, typewriting and English, eventually being successful in advanced examinations in all subjects, my grounding in office work was tough. Having spelled the word "separate" incorrectly in more than one letter, Mr. Pope announced, "If you spell 'separately' wrongly once more, I shall put up a large notice in the office which says 'Miss Wood can't spell separately'."

From that day onwards my spelling improved because a dictionary became my constant companion.

Another attraction of working for a local builder was the presence of several young craft apprentices. Being the only female in the firm, I was thoroughly spoiled by the men and the butt of practical jokes from the apprentices, many of whom I took a shine to. One of these apprentices became a very firm friend but any suggestion of him becoming my serious boyfriend was squashed by my mother over an incident about his motorbike.

I announced one Sunday afternoon that I was going out with Brian from work.

"Where are you going?" Mum enquired.

"Just for a spin on his motorbike," I replied.

"Oh not you're not, my girl. Motorbikes are death traps. You needn't think I am going to allow you on the back of the bike of a boy I don't even know!"

"But, Mum, he's waiting for me at the end of the street."

"I don't care. Go and tell him you can't go out."

I must have been seventeen years of age, yet I submissively walked to the end of the street and explained that I was not allowed to keep our date. Needless to say, Brian was not overjoyed at being stood up in this fashion. I have to admit, however, that Mum was probably right for a couple of weeks later Brian came into work with severe scratches on face, hands and arms. His explanation — he had swerved off the road catapulting himself and the girl on the pillion through a hedge.

On reflection, my four years at Pope Bros. was a period when I was very happy. The work was interesting, the camaraderie of the rest of the staff enjoyable and my boss, one of the senior partners, was fair and appreciative.

Although the war in Europe ended in May 1945 and the final hostilities ceased in June 1946, Britain still experienced rationing and shortage of many goods for several more years. I remember the particularly harsh weather of the winter of 1947. It was impossible to cycle to work on frozen roads or through deep snow drifts, so I travelled by bus and had to take a packed lunch.

Electricity for heating was also in short supply and offices, factories and homes suffered endless power cuts. At times it was too cold to operate a typewriter.

"I've had enough of this," remarked Mr Pope, my boss. "Pack up all you need for doing your work and put it in my car. We're going home to work. At least the wife has a coal fire for heating."

Thus it was that I spent several days working on the dining room table of my boss's house, rather than in the freezing cold office.

Although I had elected to continue my education after the statutory leaving age of 14 years by attending Day Commercial Classes, like my fellow students I enrolled for evening classes studying shorthand, typewriting and English. Classes were held at the College from 7–9 p.m. on three evenings of the week. After a long day in the office this could have been arduous but for the enjoyment of meeting old friends from the day course and, of course, lots of boys who studied at similar evening classes to supplement their trade apprenticeships with formal City and Guilds qualifications.

Besides the social attraction of attending these classes, there was the all-important preparation for advanced qualifications. In two years of evening classes I had passed the advanced Royal Society of Arts examinations in all three subjects and wanted to achieve my initial goal of a Typewriting Teacher's Diploma.

The College in Swindon had introduced a course to train students for the IPS (Incorporated Phonographic

Society) Typewriting Teachers' Diploma. Although not yet eighteen years of age, the minimum for entry to the examination, I was keen to attend this small group. For moral support I persuaded Kath to attend with me. She had passed her advanced typewriting examination some years previously and had several years' experience as a secretary.

The course was tough, including the principles of teaching, preparation and delivery of practical lessons as well as advanced typewriting skills.

Kath took everything in her stride, doing the minimum of work. Two weeks before the examination date in the summer of 1948, she asked to borrow my file to do some revision. Imagine my horror when the results of the examination were announced. She had passed. I failed.

Undaunted by this minor setback, I revised on my own and re-entered for the examination the following year. As there was no course at the College, I had to go to London to take the examination. Not being used to travelling in that city, I managed to arrive just five minutes before the examination commenced. I was ushered into a crowded room which must have contained nearly a hundred typewriters arranged in double rows on long tables. The room seemed to be full and the noise of practising candidates was deafening.

The invigilator greeted me with, "There's just two spare machines. Take your pick."

I settled on an L C Smith machine similar to the first one I had used at Day Commercial Classes and, within seconds, was pounding away at the first test — speed and accuracy. The examination lasted all day. The morning's practical tests of typewriting skills were arduous, each task being timed to the last minute. No time to think, look over, correct. It was a case of get it right the first time or fail.

The afternoon was dedicated to the principles of teaching. A welcome silence reigned as we all wrote the answers to this paper, during which time we were called out individually to take the practical lesson.

My examiner asked me to give a first lesson on legal documents. She explained that she would act as the student and might ask questions. I began my lesson giving clear instructions, using the chalk board and answering her simple, often repetitive, questions. All seemed to be going well until yet another repeated question was asked. In desperation I answered, "I've just explained that point. I suggest you might try paying a little more attention."

I thought, "I've blown it now", but the examiner smiled at me and commented, "Very good. I think I've seen enough. You've done well."

A practical demonstration, indicating my ability to use an ink duplicator, ended the practical section of the examination and I returned to finish the written paper.

The "Pass" slip and subsequent elaborate certificate confirming that I was now a qualified teacher of typewriting was much appreciated, although I still had in mind my ambition to be a professional actress.

CHAPTER
ELEVEN

Life's Not All Work

During the first half of the 20th century, there were no computer games to fill the leisure hours of young people. Few households possessed a television set. Hence, as children grew into teenagers, they replaced the games of their childhood with genuine hobbies. My family was no exception.

I had joined the Brownies at the age of seven and progressed to Girl Guides at the age of eleven. Kath and Win had both been Girl Guides and Win volunteered to start the Holy Rood Brownies Pack in the 1940s. I eventually assisted her by becoming Pack Leader when I was 14 years old.

As the war was still on for much of this time there were no weekly camps organized. I did attend a one-day camp whilst in the Guides. The sight of the creepy crawlies which invaded our not-too-hastily erected tent and the need to use the latrines which were hastily dug convinced me that camping was an experience I could do without.

Cycling was not only a necessary method of travelling to school and work, it was a great pastime. With very little car ownership, roads were relatively empty. Children quickly learned the rules of the road from parents who appreciated the necessity of their children having their own means of transport. By the age of eleven most children had acquired a bicycle of sorts, often as an incentive to passing the grammar school test. My parents had never agreed with such bribery so I was still riding a junior sized bicycle when Win went to teacher training college in 1941. I was promised her BSA bicycle with a three-speed gear box whilst she was away. To my utter disappointment, within two weeks of being at College, Win sent an urgent plea to have her bicycle sent on to her in Bristol since most of the girls at college had taken their bicycles with them.

Seeing my disappointment and realizing the promise they had made, my parents went out and bought me a full sized new bicycle. At the time I felt this was justified but, on reflection, I appreciate how difficult it would have been for them to find the money for this unexpected expense.

Cycling became my major form of transport and cycling became one of my hobbies. I recall many a long cycle ride with friends and family. In spring we went to the bluebell woods at Binal. In August we went blackberrying. Mum had a bicycle but was not keen on riding so most of my outings were with Dad, Win, or friends. Kath and Bill had a tandem and often took me along with them on their weekend trips.

In school holidays I would set off with a few friends for a day out. We often cycled to Cirencester to call on

Auntie Marty who worked in Mitchells — a local large draper's.

"Hello, Margaret. Fancy seeing you," would be her greeting. "I'll be home for lunch at one o'clock if you need something to eat."

"No, it's all right. We've got sandwiches and lemonade. We'll go round to City Bank to play on the swings, have a picnic and go home."

The fact that the round trip was some 30 miles with the long Blunsdon Hill to be negotiated was no deterrent. Indeed, we looked forward to ascending Blunsdon Hill on the return trip. We had competitions to see who could get the furthest up the hill before having to get off and push. Those with gears on their bikes had a distinct advantage!

Other favourite haunts were Uffington with access to the White Horse, Wayland Smithy Cave and the Ridgeway. Indeed, we gained an awful lot of local history knowledge from our countless cycle rides.

Physical exercise and sport in general provided young people with countless hours of pleasure. Most children learned to swim as the schools usually organized swimming lessons, held at the local swimming baths, for all primary school children, at least until they were able to swim.

When I left Even Swindon School to go to Holy Rood School, I was still not able to swim so continued with the weekly school swimming lessons at Holy Rood. I remember being paired with a girl who was a class or two above me and was helping out with the learners. Her name was Zena and she was very patient and helpful in encouraging me. She would stand a little way in front of me and encourage me with, "Come, on, feet off the bottom and swim towards me."

The trouble was that the unfortunate girl had a caste in one eye so I was never sure that she was looking at me. I constantly looked behind me to see who she was talking to. Although I eventually learned to swim, I never joined a swimming club or took more advanced lessons, unlike my two sisters. Maybe it was because I hated getting my face wet!

Most of my peers were goods swimmers and, in the summer holidays, they would be allowed to go swimming either at the local Milton Road swimming baths, at Coate Water, or at local gravel pits.

"Can I go swimming this afternoon, Dad?" I had been waiting patiently at the garden gate for him to come home to lunch.

"I don't see why not," was his reply. Dad was an excellent swimmer and saw no fear in water. I skipped up the path ahead of him to announce to Mum, who had already refused her permission, "Dad said I can go swimming."

"What's the point of my saying 'No' if you are going to counteract it?" queried Mum.

"I didn't know you had said 'No' when she asked" explained Dad.

That lunchtime was taken up with arguments between Mum and Dad. Fortunately, for my safety, Mum won and I was not allowed to go to the local gravel pits with my friends.

Ah, well, my ploy didn't work that time, but . . . next time!

Having played hockey at school, Win joined a local hockey club called Moredon Ladies Hockey Club. By the age of fourteen I also became a member, rising to Match Secretary some three years later.

There was an active Wiltshire County Hockey team for whom Win played and a well-supported Swindon Hockey league to which Moredon Ladies team belonged. In the winter, Saturday afternoons were taken up with friendly or league matches. Once a year there was a six-a-side tournament.

Our pitch was at Maundrell's farm in Moredon, a field kindly loaned to us by the farmer. Each Saturday a few members of the team had to arrive early to collect and erect the goal posts and to check for, and clear, the remnants of cow pats. The farmer used the field for grazing his cattle during the rest of the week. The other drawback to this venue was that the field had quite a slope on it. Visiting teams soon got wise to electing to play uphill for the first half when players were fresh.

"I do wish you would give up this dangerous sport," Mum would say as we hobbled home from our Saturday afternoon escapades, seeking methylated spirits to put on our bruises. I recall coming home with a black eye after one match. A high-flying ball had caught me off guard. The scar was the subject of much conversation for some days.

I guess I was about fifteen years old when Kath introduced me to ballroom dancing. She and our next-door neighbour, Mrs. Stafford, had joined

Rodbourne Community Centre where an Old Time Dancing group met. The weekly meetings were well-attended and great fun. I soon picked up such dances as the Military Two Step, the Gay Gordons and square dances such as the Lancers and the Quadrilles. The annual balls held by the group afforded a chance to dress in proper ball gowns (inevitably made by Mum) and to engage in the etiquette of a bygone era.

With evening classes three times a week, choir practice, elocution lessons, weekly hockey matches in the winter and tennis and swimming in the summer, there was little time to visit the cinema or theatre but I still had my dream. One day I would be "treading the boards", one day my name would be up there in lights. Fuelled with this determination I seized every possible opportunity of going to the local Playhouse Theatre to see the productions of the repertory company or local amateur dramatic groups. Later I even managed the odd Saturday in London to see a West End production.

I still remained convinced that one day my dream would be fulfilled.

CHAPTER
TWELVE

The Dream Becomes
a Hobby

The foundation and growth of Youth Clubs were phenomena of the immediate post-war years — the late 1940s. Held in local school buildings, they provided a recreational base for young people to meet new friends, socialize and join in the various activities on offer.

By 1946, I was sixteen years of age. The war was over and life was beginning to return to normal. There were no disruptions in the form of air raid warnings, so people began to think about regaining their social lives.

Like most of my peers, I joined a Youth Club. I chose Westcott Youth Centre as it had a thriving amateur dramatic society run by a talented amateur actor, Walter Webb. We met once a week and I became friendly with several young thespians, most of whom were equally talented and some even dreaming of a career in the theatre. I felt I was in good company and I learned a lot about stagecraft in those early years. The group entered many one-act play festivals and soon learned to take criticism.

The most important attribute of my joining Westcott Youth Centre was that I met my first serious boy friend, Alex Worster. Alex was a keen amateur actor and very talented. Wally Webb appreciated his talent and gave him extra coaching and many good parts in plays. Truth to tell I became jealous of Wally's interest in Alex.

Together with other members of the group, we joined another amateur dramatic group trying to establish itself — the St. Augustine Players. This group was formed by parishioners from a local church in Rodbourne. The producer was Evelyn Albinson, a spinster school teacher who was a competent producer but with little sense of humour. Many are the times we had to be admonished for lack of diligence to the job in hand. Her warning, "Do you realize it's only two weeks to production," usually ensured we got down to serious rehearsals. St. Augustine Players aimed to put on at least two three-act plays during the year.

Although several members of the Westcott Youth Centre drama group joined St. Augustine Players, they did not stay long. Only the really dedicated participants continued for several years. Other members were drawn from the congregation and local residents. I made many friends and enjoyed some really good castings from that group. The fact that I usually got the female juvenile lead gave me scope to develop my talent. We had great fun performing both dramas, such as *The Ghost Train, Peril at End House, Rebecca, Dark Victory* and *A Murder Has Been Arranged* as well as comedies such as *Money by Wire, Acacia Avenue, The Lady Purrs* and *The Blue Goose.*

136

It seemed now that all my free time was taken up with amateur dramatics and elocution lessons. These ensured I got several solo spots in concerts given by the AEU choir which I had joined with Win and Dad.

My circle of friends was expanding and Alex and I were together most evenings, sharing our love of acting. At weekends we went for cycle rides or to the cinema or even stayed at home, listening to the plays of Shakespeare on the gramophone. Alex accompanied my family on several seaside holidays. With the end of the war families soon returned to their annual "trip" holidays at a coastal resort.

Whilst I was still attending evening classes studying shorthand, typewriting and English two or three times a week, Alex was extending his amateur acting and, largely through Wally's influence, was introduced to other local groups, not least the Civic Shakespeare group. With parts for men being in abundance and having a developing talent he soon got offered more and more parts. I eventually was selected for minor parts in civic productions and became more and more aware of the competition from other talented thespians. I was still keen to achieve recognition for any acting talents and to enjoy performing various parts, but I was doing well at evening classes, enjoyed my work as a secretary and had a serious boyfriend. My dream of becoming a professional actress was fading.

By 1949 I had ceased being a student at evening classes. Having gained my Typewriting Teachers' Diploma in November 1949, I was offered a post as a tutor of an intermediate typewriting evening class at the College for the following year — September 1950.

The preliminary staff meeting was conducted by Mr. Sladen, Head of Commerce and my old head teacher whilst I was a Day Commercial Classes. We were told about the various administrative procedures to be undertaken and warned that, "Students expect to be entered for external examinations. Naturally they expect to pass. Indeed, if they fail, you can hold yourselves responsible."

Thus it was that I entered, nervously, on my first teaching experience, knowing that failure would almost certainly mean that I would not be offered another class. But failure was not something that I ever seriously contemplated. I knew I would have to prepare my lessons meticulously but had every confidence in my ability.

The evening of my first class approached. I decided to get to the College about an hour beforehand so that I could locate the room, familiarize myself with the typewriters and collect the class register, etc.

"I'm here for the intermediate typewriting class," I announced to the receptionist.

"You'll need to register first," she replied, thrusting a form into my hand.

I took the form, perused it and then returned to the reception desk.

"I'm the teacher, not a potential student. What I need is the register, not an enrolment form."

Her look of disdain was enough to convince me that my youthful looks were not going to be an advantage in teaching adults. I decided to put some theory notes on the blackboard so that students had something to occupy them whilst I helped sort out the typewriters. I hardly thought it fit to use the same procedure for allocating machines as "Fossy" had used for my own first typing lesson. Most of my students were already in employment. None of them were beginners. They would know which machines they wanted. I just prayed that there would be enough different makes to satisfy them and there would be no squabbling.

The students began to arrive and by 7p.m. I had a class of about twenty, mostly settled at machines of their choice. I suggested they copy the notes from the blackboard whilst we waited for any latecomers. Only a few began the task. Fearing a rebellion about to erupt, I enquired of students at the back of the class why they weren't writing.

"We can't read what you've written," was the reply.

Sure enough, anyone sitting beyond the first two rows was unable to decipher the minutely handwritten notes so patiently put on the board before the lesson. This was my initiation into the motto of any teacher — be prepared.

I quickly changed my lesson plan, beginning with a practical test and leaving the theory notes until after the break, during which time I would rewrite them in a larger hand!

I enjoyed this first teaching experience and, being successful (or rather ensuring my students were successful at their external examinations), I was offered an advanced class the next year. The syllabus to be followed meant that I had to teach stencil cutting and ink duplicating. I approached these tasks confidently with well-prepared lesson plans. After a few lessons I was ready to demonstrate ink duplicating using the new modern electric duplicator. The lesson began. I plugged in the duplicator and the whole college was plunged into darkness. The electricity supply had failed. Classes were halted and students sent home.

I was somewhat annoyed at having to postpone my planned demonstration until the following week. In the staff room, the cause of the blackout was being investigated. It appeared that someone had plugged an AC appliance into a DC electrical socket. Someone in one of the ground floor rooms. That was funny. My classroom was on the ground floor.

Not considering the need to be a qualified electrician before using equipment, I never admitted that, on checking sockets the next lesson, I had been the cause of the chaos.

After a couple of years teaching typewriting to evening class students, I realized that although my first love remained the theatre, my parents had been right when they persuaded me to study some "bread and butter" subjects. My evening classes provided a welcome addition to my salary as a secretary and, what was more important, I was enjoying the work.

Acting was still a vital part of my life but maybe it was time to get things into perspective — amateur dramatics was just a hobby.

CHAPTER
THIRTEEN

Change of Career

Teaching evening classes made me contemplate a career as a teacher, but having failed the eleven plus examination and therefore not having a grammar school education with its resultant opportunity to matriculate, I was not able to follow the conventional teacher training route.

Fired with enthusiasm and with a Typewriting Teachers' Diploma in hand, I vowed that I would not be deterred — I would teach, however difficult it may be to gain full recognition. I decided that probably the most rewarding for me, as a teacher, would be from teaching privately. I figured that if students, or their parents, were paying for the tuition they would be keen to progress and I would gain satisfaction from their achievements.

I borrowed £20 from my sister Win, bought a secondhand LC Smith typewriter and started teaching in my parents' front room. Local advertising and word of mouth recommendations soon meant I had more pupils than I could cope with individually, so I borrowed more money from my sister and bought first a portable typewriter and then another full-size machine. I could now teach three students at a time. I charged them two shillings an hour each and soon managed to repay my debts to Win.

At this time there was a great demand for shorthand and typewriting tuition since these subjects were rarely taught in secondary schools and, for those pupils who had failed the 11+, these skills opened the doors to office jobs, rather than factory work.

Teaching privately gave me the experience of teaching various age groups. I was used to the adults, many of whom had spent the day at work or looking after children and doing household chores. They longed to return to work or to progress to a better job and saw office skills as their opportunity. They worked tirelessly and were demanding in their need to progress swiftly.

It was clear to me that, if I was to develop the business further, I needed to be able to teach shorthand as well as typewriting. I had never enjoyed shorthand when I was at Day Commercial Classes and it was always a "penance" for me to continue shorthand lessons at evening classes until I had gained my Advanced shorthand examination. Indeed, I had always maintained that I hated learning shorthand so much, I would never teach it since I would feel too sorry for the pupils. But this was a necessity. If I was going to teach, eventually full-time, I would have to offer more than one subject.

I set about revising the theory of shorthand and followed a correspondence course. It was not easy but I eventually gained the RSA Teachers' Diploma in

142

Pitman's Shorthand although I did not begin teaching it until 1951.

During this time I tried to keep up my other interests. My elocution lessons had ensured my success at the London Academy of Dramatic Art Gold Medal examination and I was determined to continue until I had gained my Associateship (ALAM) in elocution.

I still played hockey every Saturday during the winter and acted as the club's match secretary. Although not professing to be a chorister, I attended choir practice once a week, since the AEU choir gave many local concerts and I was always selected for a solo spot, either reciting a poem or a scene from a play.

Alex and I still belonged to amateur dramatic groups but whilst he was keen on developing his already considerable talent, I was branching out into other activities. Sadly, after some two or three years together, Alex and I parted.

I had now been working as a secretary to Pope Bros., local builders, for some three years and was quite happy until I heard that the nearby RAF station, which had been leased to the American Air Force, were looking for a teacher of shorthand and typewriting.

This was the opportunity I had been waiting for and I grabbed it with both hands. I went for an interview at the base. Apart from the war years, this was my first encounter with Americans, or army personnel.

"We need you to teach four two-hour sessions a day, Monday to Friday," the interviewing Captain explained.

I was used to teaching two-hour sessions at evening classes so this posed no threat to me.

143

"Fine," I replied. "Who would be my students?"

"They would all be army or air force personnel. Some would already be working as clerical officers so you would need to familiarize yourself with the layout of official army documents so that you could teach that aspect of typewriting."

"No problems. Just tell me where I can get such information," I replied, somewhat over-confidently.

I was offered the post at a fabulous salary, some four times what I was earning as a secretary (albeit the hours were much longer), given an armful of books and papers and had my daily transport arranged from Swindon to Fairford. I looked forward to my first class at 8 a.m. the following Monday. The transport arrangements were with an army sergeant who was living with his family in Swindon and travelled, by car, to the base each day. There was one slight problem. He left at 7 a.m. and I had to cycle to his house in the centre of town. It was a long day. My last class finished at 5 p.m. but that was not the time I left the base. My sergeant would usually call in at the PX in order to purchase liquid refreshments. The journey home was quite hazardous. I held the uncorked whiskey bottle whilst he was driving. He would then take regular swigs from the proffered bottle.

Before my first class, I was shown the layout of the relevant sections of the base and told that, as I was the only female at present on the base, a toilet had been allocated for me and suitably labelled "Ladies". My first visit to the toilet was somewhat of a rude awakening. I opened the door to be greeted by an RAF airman sitting on the toilet with his trousers round his ankles.

I don't know who was the most embarrassed but I was sufficiently annoyed to ask, "What on earth do you think you are doing? Can't you read the notice?"

A very confused and apologetic young man explained, "Sorry. I thought the notice was joke since there are no women on the base and I was just fed up using the other disgusting toilets."

Apology accepted, he scurried off and I never saw him again. I did, however, insist on having a key for my toilet.

The first morning's lessons came and went with little hitch. The men were well disciplined and seemed keen to attend lessons since it was often a "soft option" compared to their normal allotted tasks. The last lesson of each afternoon was set aside for shorthand tuition. It would be my first venture of teaching shorthand but I was not too worried. I was well into my correspondence course for my Teachers' Diploma and, as usual, had planned a good introductory lesson. The students filed in, some 15 to 20 in all but this time many of them from senior ranks and office personnel.

I started my introduction. It appeared some already had a knowledge of shorthand so maybe all that was needed was a refresher course.

"Excuse me, Ma'am," one young man ventured early in the lesson. "We don't seem to be speaking the same language. What system of shorthand are you teaching?"

"Why, Pitman's, of course."

"That's no good to us. In the USA Gregg's shorthand is the most prevalent. Very few office personnel use Pitman's. Can't you teach us Gregg's?"

I had a good knowledge of other forms of shorthand since I had toyed with the idea of finding a less difficult system than Pitman's to learn myself.

"Well, I don't know the system very well, so would have to keep a couple of lessons ahead of you but I'm willing to have a go."

"Fine, that's what we will do," they all agreed.

Maybe this time I was being just a little bit over-confident! I tried hard, so did the students, but class numbers dwindled so rapidly that the class became uneconomical and it was decided that I should teach general office administration rather than shorthand for the last lesson of each day.

The typewriting lessons proved no difficulty for me. The authorities had hired twenty Underwood typewriters, all the same model. How easy it became to teach on one model rather than the multiplicity of machines at the local college or for my private pupils!

In an early morning class there was a student named Sergeant Wright. He was always late for class and the fact that one could often see the bottom of his pyjama trousers showing beneath his uniform, suggested he was not an early riser. He was also prone to angry outbursts. One day, whilst executing a rather difficult piece of display work he stood up and shouted, "These bloody Limey typewriters."

Thinking the next action would be his throwing the said machine through the nearby window, I decided to

146

take swift action. I walked hurriedly to his place in the class, took him by the arm, (he was now standing), marched him round to the back of the desk and pointed to the back of the typewriter on which was written, "Made in USA".

I had no more problems with Sergeant Wright. He learned to control his temper in my presence but I fear his fellow students suffered from his "short fuse".

It transpired that very few of my students worked in clerical jobs. The US Air Force had just taken over the base from the RAF and they needed to extend the runway in order to accommodate their large aircraft. They also needed to train personnel to do an ever-increasing amount of clerical work. Personnel were directed from labouring work into my classes so that they could be trained as shorthand typists.

There were several problems with this philosophy. Firstly, those who were in the army to do labouring work were usually not the best educated. Some were barely literate. Added to this they arrived at my typewriting classes with cement-caked fingers that were already too large to fit on the conventional keyboards. There was also the race problem. Blacks and whites did not mix. All the white men came in first and sat in the front rows. The black men occupied what seats were left, always at the back of the class. I must say that those seated in the back rows were the most industrious and caused me few problems.

The army provided a bus into Swindon early evening so that the soldiers and airmen could take some leave off base. With classes finishing at 5p.m., it was almost impossible to get changed and be ready for the bus into town, hence I was often bribed to let a student leave early. I was not overtly open to intimidation, but I did receive quite a few boxes of chocolates during my time at Fairford.

I have never worked so hard in my life but I enjoyed the work, the environment, my accepted status as a professional and the fact that I knew that teaching was something I could do for the rest of my life — though not for the US Air Force. I found the Americans over-powering and fanatically patriotic. I grew tired of being told I must visit America, it was such a marvellous country. After enduring years of worn-torn Britain, I was quite happy to wait until my own country could get back on its feet. "Paradise" (in the terms of America) could wait a while.

Something else was happening in my life. I had been without a boyfriend for some months and was missing the attention of the opposite sex. I answered an invitation for a pen pal in a Catholic newspaper and soon started writing to a young man called Peter Gane who, although from London, was doing his national service in the RAF in Norfolk. Would this mean things were going to change for me?

CHAPTER
FOURTEEN

Goodbye Swindon

Having no boyfriend for a period enabled me to concentrate on my new career in teaching. Although the days were long, working at the US Air Base at Fairford, I still managed to keep an evening or two free for amateur dramatics and choir practice. I also continued, in the winter months, with my typewriting evening class at The College and with my growing band of private pupils who now encroached into my weekends because I taught on a Saturday morning.

About this time the Youth Clubs were developing and offering academic classes in addition to social activities. I was offered a shorthand class which was attached to St. Joseph's Secondary School.

Teaching in a Youth Centre brought new challenges. Classes had to compete with such interesting activities as table tennis, football training etc. Students were largely drawn from the local area and were still of school age. To keep their interest in such an academic and demanding subject as shorthand meant planning the lessons so that the most interesting part was left until after break time. Trying to persuade them to return from a ten-minute break on time was another problem, but we pressed on and a number of children achieved much success, and possibly a change in career prospects, from the classes.

A number of pupils were of Polish extraction, their parents having fled Poland during the war years and settled in Swindon. Their knowledge of English was not always very good but, as shorthand was a phonetic system, they were able to take dictation and read back what they had written, although not always understanding the subject matter. These students were most diligent in their studies.

I was now getting a taste for teaching shorthand and before long I was asked to take a shorthand class at The College. I remember arriving in the staff room to be greeted by one of my old shorthand teachers from evening classes. When I told him I was teaching an intermediate class he exploded with laughter.

"I hope you know a bit more theory than when you were in my class," he remarked.

"I've almost completed a correspondence course for a Teachers' Diploma," I replied.

"I thought you hated shorthand. You always made hard work of my lessons."

I explained that I was already teaching typewriting both at the College and privately and was teaching full-time at Fairford. I knew that to progress further I would have to teach shorthand as well. The fact that I was never keen to learn the subject and had found it hard work was not going to deter me from teaching it. He wished me luck and introduced me to the rest of the staff.

150

Before the lesson we were informed that the wife of the Director of Education for Swindon was taking shorthand lessons as a refresher course and could well be in one of our classes. My heart sank when I noticed her name on my register.

As usual the lesson was well-planned and I confidently wrote outlines on the board for difficult words, explaining the application of theoretical points. To my horror, Mrs. Jellicoe (the VIP of the class) and her friends frequently questioned the accuracy of my outlines. I was determined not to let any student shake my confidence. There must be an explanation for our conflicting outlines.

During the break I approached Mrs. Jellicoe and her friends with some trepidation. Apologising for the fact that we seemed to be at variance, I questioned, "Can I ask when you first learned shorthand."

"At school."

"Would that have been some years ago?" I queried.

"Of course."

"Then you are probably using the original 'classic' shorthand outlines. The system was completely revised in the early 1940s and a new version called the New Era system was brought out. We are using the new version here."

Fortunately my grandfather, father and aunts had all learned the classic, original system devised by Sir Isaac Pitman (from whom my grandfather had received his Teachers' Certificate) and I had used their original textbooks and read lots of their notes so I could spot the differences. The ladies in question accepted my

151

explanation and seemed impressed with my knowledge of both the classic and New Era versions.

By this time, the letters to my RAF pen pal, Peter, had become more and more prolific until, after about three months, he suggested we meet one weekend. As his home was in London we agreed to meet at Paddington Station and spend the weekend at his grandmother's house in north-west London. Once again my mother had other ideas.

"You are not going to London to meet some boy you don't know," she announced.

"But I do know him. We've been writing to each other for weeks," I pleaded.

"I don't care. I don't know him. If you want to meet it will be here, under our roof."

Although then twenty years old, I again meekly agreed with my mother and Peter started visiting me in Swindon most weekends. My parents got to know him. Dad liked him but, although Mum welcomed him to her home and even offered to do his washing each weekend, she never really took to him.

"There's something not quite right about him," she would say.

However, love is blind. We fell for each other in a big way. Peter said that he would be finishing his national service in January so we decided, much to our parents' disappointment, to get married on December 15th. The wedding was at Holy Rood Church with Win as my bridesmaid. My poor father was in hospital, having sustained a burst stomach ulcer the week before, so Kath's husband Bill, gave me away. With Peter's leave

152

from the RAF arranged, Dad had insisted that the wedding go ahead as planned. Peter and I went to visit him straight from the ceremony. At the sight of me in my wedding dress, Dad burst into tears. He was very ill and I had never seen him cry before. I won't say the visit spoilt my day but I certainly never forgot the sight of him in tears.

We spent a week in London as a honeymoon and returned to my home for the few days of Christmas, then Peter had to go back to camp.

The custom in the 1950s was that the wife followed her husband as regards making a home. Peter was due to be demobbed in January and had his old job at Paddington Town Hall awaiting him, so it was time to make a move. Housing was in short supply so soon after the war, especially in London which had lost large swathes of its housing stock in the air raids. Thus it was that we started married life in a bed-sitter in his grandmother's rented house in Neasden, north-west London. Peter managed to get the RAF to agree to his living out, so he travelled daily to his camp which was now at Stanmore.

It had been hard for me to give up my successful life in Swindon. The personnel at Fairford said they were sad to see me go and both staff and students gave me a good send-off with many wedding presents. I also had a good reference which I could use to further my teaching career, if I so desired.

My private pupils either enrolled at evening classes or found another private tutor. At this time, one of my private pupils, Joan Rumming, had reached Teachers'

Diploma standard with me and she set up a small school in premises in Bath Road and took most of my pupils.

My biggest disappointment was leaving St. Augustine Players but they all wished me well and off I went to a new life in London.

Peter knew that my first love was the theatre and that I had always had the dream of becoming a professional actress. This dream, he said, could best be achieved in London. I believed him and started my married life "on a high".

Of one thing I am certain, the year 1951 was to set the stamp on my compulsion for hard work. From that period I became a workaholic and guess I will remain so until my dying day. Whether this is a good or bad thing can be judged from reading about the rest of my life.

Also available in ISIS Large Print:

Aintree Days

Alexander Tulloch

If the sound of Sunday was church bells, the smell of Sunday was cabbage.

Alexander Tulloch effortlessly evokes life in Liverpool from 1945 to 1962, when he was growing up with his parents, sister and grandparents in a small terraced house in Aintree. He conjures up a world, to today's children as alien as Victorian England, in which all adults seemed to smoke for England, a pint of beer cost a few pence, where frost painted patterns on the inside of windows every winter, where the "lav" was a trek across the yard and where you always went on holiday to Landudno — an exciting 60 miles away.

ISBN 978-0-7531-9430-0 (hb)
ISBN 978-0-7531-9431-7 (pb)

For What It's Worth

Bryan Kelly

"I was a fledgling Liver-Bird fluttering its unaccustomed wings, ready to soar blindly into the beckoning future, unaware of its apparent pitfalls and dangers."

Bryan Kelly was born in 1931. His father was a docker, and he and his seven brothers and sisters grew up in a tiny terraced house in Anfield. Although life for Bryan and his family was hard, he recalls his time growing up with great fondness. With recollections of schooldays, local characters, wartime (and particularly the Blitz), church activities and recreation, as well as anecdotes from day-to-day family life, this book is sure to conjure up many nostalgic memories for all those who know and love the city of Liverpool.

ISBN 978-0-7531-9412-6 (hb)
ISBN 978-0-7531-9413-3 (pb)